"Maurice's street savvy gives him instant credibility with children of all ages. I never tire of watching a roomful of kids who have absolutely no interest in chess light up as Maurice tells his story. His ideas change lives and need to be heard. Invest in your child's future; buy this book today."

—*Cris Collinsworth, four-time Emmy Award–winning broadcaster*

"This book is inspirational, informative, well written—and will no doubt spur on many youngsters to attempt to emulate Maurice Ashley's remarkable success in chess and life."

—*Gregory H. Williams, President of the City College of New York*

"Maurice continues to demonstrate the qualities of leadership and innovation which have characterized his chess career."

—*Erik Anderson, Founder of America's Foundation for Chess*

BROADWAY BOOKS

NEW YORK

CHESS
for
SUCCESS

Using an Old Game to
Build New Strengths in
Children and Teens

MAURICE ASHLEY
International Chess Grandmaster

PRINTED IN THE UNITED STATES OF AMERICA

BROADWAY BOOKS and its logo, a letter B bisected on the diagonal,
are trademarks of Random House, Inc.

Visit our website at www.broadwaybooks.com

First edition published 2005.

Book design by Jennifer Ann Daddio

Library of Congress Cataloging-in-Publication Data

Ashley, Maurice.
Chess for success : using an old game to build new strengths in
children and teens / Maurice Ashley.— 1st ed.
p. cm.
1. Chess. 2. Personality development. 3. Success in adolescence.
I. Title.

GV1318.A79 2004
2004061779

ISBN 0-7679-1568-2

1   3   5   7   9   10   8   6   4   2

FOR NIA AND JAYDEN

CONTENTS

ACKNOWLEDGMENTS

This book would never have been possible without the love, support, creative insight, and patience of many. To the people listed here: You know how passionately I express myself. Keep that in mind as you read my words of appreciation for how you have helped me complete this task, and, in most cases, contributed to the person I am. I can only begin to convey my gratitude. Thank you all.

Thanks . . .

To my mother, Thelma Cormack, for making the hard decision of being separate from your children in order to make a better life for us. Every goal I achieve is a living testament to the success of your foresight. I hope to never waste your sacrifice.

To my grandmother, Irma Cormack, for taking a decade out of your life to raise your three grandkids. I miss you more as I get older, and I only wish I had gotten to say good-bye. Thank you, Mama.

To my brother Devon and the *rude boys* from Tower Hill in Jamaica, for getting me started on this wonderful chess journey.

To my dad, for stepping up and being a caring force in

your children's lives. Thanks for letting me bug you into buying all those chess books.

To Vincent "Leon" Munro, for being there during the Rockaway Parkway years. With all those early emotional times, I'm glad we are still friends more than twenty years later.

To my agent, Linda Konner, for believing that I could pull this off, even when I gave you plenty of reasons not to.

To Valerie Bohigian, for letting go of your original idea, and letting me run with a project for which you felt so much passion. I hope I was able to adequately represent your vision.

To Doubleday/Broadway vice president Janet Hill, for having the faith and confidence to support my message when others didn't want to take a chance on the project.

To my editor, Clarence Haynes, for being so patient with my crazy schedule. Thanks for taking the heat for my lateness.

To Big Vicky and Lil' Vickie, for looking after the baby so I could have time to write.

To my high school friend Clotaire Colas, for being such a great rival.

To Zenaida Grenald, my assistant, who kept me sane when the details threatened to overwhelm.

To Betty Deichman, for seeing my potential and getting me my first job as a chess coach. I miss your smile and wry sense of humor.

To Courtney Welch, who was the best boss and warmest friend anyone could ever hope for. I will always be grateful.

To Willie Johnson, for being like a father to me. You are a great friend, confidant, spiritual guide, chess coach, and, most of all, patient listener. Thanks for never once letting me stay down.

To all the warriors of the Black Bear School (Ronald Simpson, William Morrison, Chris Welcome, Herminio Baez, as well as the late George Golden and Mark Meeres). Your viciously intense, no-holds-barred, knock-down, drag-out fighting style prepared me for the rigorous world of competitive chess.

To my great friend Josh Waitzkin. Our treks over the world fighting all those chess wars were some of the best times of my life. Budapest and Bad Wiessee had never seen two guys like us! I love you, man.

To Dan Rose, for his emotional and financial support over the years. Without your unending faith in me, I would never have become a grandmaster. Your infectious optimism and unselfish generosity will always be a model for how I should live my life.

To all the kids whose lives I've touched and who have touched mine. You've helped me to learn that you are our greatest promise. Your spirit, determination, and youthful exuberance are always a joy to witness.

And finally, to my wife, Michele, my partner, my love. When I think it can't get any better, it does. Your affection and support are my surest constants. I feel blessed to wake up each morning next to you.

FOREWORD

I came to know Maurice Ashley when my wife, Jada, surprised me on Valentine's Day of 2000 with my very own chess lesson with a grandmaster. It takes a special wife and an insane husband to play chess on Valentine's Day. She knows the love (obsession) that I have for the game.

Maurice and I had a great time that evening, playing and talking for hours. I learned a bit about how his mind works, and about his dedication to the young people he coached. Our mutual respect has grown to this day.

My own passion for the game began at age seven when my father introduced me to the game, including the basic moves, the strategies, and then the parallels to life. He beat me ten games a week for the next seven years of my life. Then, at age fourteen, I finally saw my checkmate coming from three moves out.

I had him. I was terrified that he would see it, but happily the inevitable occurred. He looked across the board, put his hand on my shoulder, and said, "I've done my job, I can die now." Fortunately, he hasn't died yet, so he's able to witness the power of the lessons and the fruit of the seeds he has planted. Now, whenever I have a break on the set of my latest movie, I find time to rumble with one of my various chess buddies. Whether it's with Jamie Foxx or Barry Bonds, the trash-talking is always fierce. (I have an almost 100 percent kill rating over those guys. ☺) Chess has that special ability to exercise the mind while also being entertaining and exciting.

Is chess good for young people? Yes! Without question. It helps them to think better, calculate plans, set goals, develop their self-esteem, and understand the relationship between choices and repercussions. It also helps them to dvelop a unique focus that can only help them in their day-to-day lives. It's an activity that any child can participate in, no matter what his or her personal situation is, and it's something that families can do together, as my older son and I have begun to do.

The book spells out Maurice Ashley's vision for chess and its benefits for young people. He has made it his life's mission to expose as many people, young and old, to a game that has helped him so profoundly. Just reading the first chapter about his personal story helps one to see that real impact chess can have on a life. And his message that chess is great for kids comes alive with the stories of his own students and kids across the country who have benefited from the game. It's a great message of hope—that chess can be one piece of the puzzle to help our young people shine. It's what we all want for our kids.

—*Will Smith*

CHESS *for* SUCCESS

INTRODUCTION

The Power of the Game

The greatest discovery of my generation is that a human being can alter his life by altering his attitude of mind.

—WILLIAM JAMES

Improving your thinking skill is actually much, much simpler than most people believe.

—EDWARD DE BONO

A chess phenomenon is slowly spreading to schools all around the country. In classrooms where it has taken hold, educators are reporting astounding results. After learning how to play chess, kids who once showed little interest in getting a good education are not only turning their grades, and lives, around, they are excelling. Inner-city schools now sport huge chess trophies won by their students at National Championships. These same kids are going on to college at a rate far exceeding expectations, with some graduating from universities like Harvard, Yale, and Princeton. How and why chess has the power to allow students to achieve these remarkable outcomes is the subject of this book.

Numerous studies have detailed the benefits of playing chess. The list reads like a dream for parents and educators.

Chess:

- develops logical thinking
- sharpens problem-solving skills
- improves concentration and focus
- enhances imagination and creativity
- develops the capacity to foresee the consequences of one's actions
- promotes independence and a sense of responsibility
- hones memory
- heightens self-esteem
- reinforces the concept of deferred gratification and much more!

It goes without saying that the educational system needs a shot in the arm. A high percentage of kids at every grade level performs below standard every year, and a disheartening number of teenagers drop out of high school. The federal government has been desperately trying to change this sad state of affairs for decades; the merits of its latest initiative, the policy of No Child Left Behind, are still being debated.

It would be naïve of me to claim that the inclusion of chess in the curriculum is all that's needed to radically change the system. The issues of inadequate funding, lack of qualified teachers, large class size, and, in some cases, poor administrative leadership need to be addressed if true changes are to occur. What I can confidently say is that chess, like science, mathematics, and music, is a powerful tool that can help to dramatically improve the mental faculties of kids who play.

I know firsthand the transformative power of chess. It had a profound effect on me, growing up in inner-city Brooklyn. In chapter one, I tell the story of how chess set fire to my young imagination and infused me with a profound sense of purpose. My love for the game kept me from hanging out on the streets with many of my friends, and my passion for chess eventually catapulted me to attain the game's most prestigious title, International Grandmaster.

In chapter two, I give the reader a quick taste of the fascinating and varied history of chess, with all the kings, queens, politicians, and famous players who gladly fell prey to the game's intriguing charms. The chapter shows how the game has left behind its old image as a game for the wealthy and has now become a game that is played by people of all social strata.

Chapter three is an important one for those looking for scientific research that shows how and why chess works.

I give a brief review of the critical studies, and then show the intimate connection between chess and current educational theories.

In chapter four, I chronicle the real-life experiences that attest to the real power of chess. Beginning with my own experience as a chess coach, I tell the stories of the programs and kids on the front lines. Behind every story is a young person whose life has been profoundly affected by chess, in most cases told in their own words. There can be no more inspiring proof to the benefits of chess then these courageous young people.

Chapter five is for those who need some ideas on how to motivate their kids to get started. I offer a wide array of interesting tips to motivate young people, and I also discuss the super-important topic of girls and chess.

In chapter six, I touch on four of the life lessons I learned from playing chess. This could easily have been an entire book (I may write it one day), because playing and studying chess have given me an incredible number of insights on how to walk this planet.

I close the book with a number of additional tips, tools, and resources. From Frequently Asked Questions and the Basic Rules to the best books to use, interesting Web sites to visit, and a list of famous people who play chess, this section will help interested readers get well on their way to learning more about this fascinating game.

My message is a simple one: Chess is great for kids. I know how it affected my life. I have seen its effects on the kids I have coached. And I have studied an overwhelming body of evidence that powerfully shows the amazing benefits young people can gain from playing chess. In an age where flashy images rule and thirty-second messages have replaced informed thinking, the advent of chess in homes and classrooms across America could have a resounding effect on the next generation of our nation's kids.

Common Myths
About Chess

Before we go any further, I want to clear up some of the major, and sometimes damaging, misconceptions that folks generally have about chess. These false images often serve to keep some young people and adults from learning to play, while deterring others from continuing an activity that could have an enormous impact on their lives. The sooner we can root out these misconceptions, the better. So let's get started.

Myth # 1: Chess is hard to learn.

Reality: The average person can learn all the rules of chess in less than an hour. Kids as young as four years old are ready to learn to play, while most six-year-olds will have no difficulty picking up all the rules in one or, at most, two sittings.

Myth #2: Kids are intimidated by the game.

Reality: The truth is that *adults,* holding fast to the belief of myth number 1, are far more intimidated by chess than are kids. Most kids have never heard of chess before they see it for the first time, and therefore have no idea that it's somehow on a par with rocket science. To them, chess looks like a cooler version of checkers.

Myth #3: Today's kids are into PlayStation or Nintendo, and will never take to a slow game like chess.

Reality: This is one of the most pernicious myths of all because it assumes that our children are simply incapable of slowing down. Fortunately, chess educators around the country know that this is not true. Chess has a magic all its own that mystifies young people. Go to any scholastic chess tournament and you will be amazed to see hundreds of kids focused on their games. For most parents and educators seeing it for the first time, it's almost a miracle to see their children sitting quietly for more than fifteen minutes doing anything other than watching television. And yes: The kids are actually having fun!

Myth #4: Chess is for nerds.

Reality: In this country, it's generally the case that anything cerebral is thought of as nerdy. In the worst case, this even applies to getting good grades in school. This image of chess does not hold sway in most countries around the world where the game is hugely popular and gets the sort of respect soccer does. Corporations clamor to sponsor major chess tournaments because of the pluses of aligning their brands with the game's intellectual image. And up until their government fell apart, the Soviets used to give stipends to their international stars so they could play the sport full-time. It was even common for chess players to win Sportsman of the Year awards.

In the United States, the nerd image will be very difficult to shake. But when superstars like Will Smith, Jamie Foxx, and Madonna, just to name a few, show their love for the game, it might not be long before chess deservingly takes on the image of being a cool activity.

Myth #5: Chess is boring.

Reality: Those of us who play chess know that it has all the intensity of any major sport, including basketball, football, baseball, tennis, and golf. I'm a huge fan of all of these sports, and I get the same feeling watching or playing them as I do watching or playing chess. How can a game that involves sitting quietly and thinking compare to all these fast-moving activities, you ask? Isn't watching chess sort of like watching grass grow? Sure, if you don't know what's going on. But for the avid chess player, the excruciating tension of an important game is more like watching your wife go through labor. (My wife went through sixty hours with our daughter, so I know of what I speak!)

Myth #6: Chess players are crazy.

Reality: Well, I have met a few chess players who might fit this description. No doubt, where there is genius, there is sometimes madness (witness John Nash from the book and movie *A Beautiful Mind*). American World Champion Bobby Fischer, with his many eccentricities and severe paranoia, only reinforced this perception.

Naturally, as often happens, famous people in an activity tend to dictate the public's image of the rest of the practitioners. Still, most people would not make the mistake of thinking that all tennis players love fashion design because Venus and Serena Williams do. With the public knowing so little about chess, there is the powerful tendency to generalize on meager evidence. The reality is that the vast majority of chess players do not fit this stigma at all.

Myth #7: Chess is just a game and has no redeeming social value. We might as well teach kids Parcheesi.

Reality: I don't want to rile all the Parcheesi lovers out there, but chess is most definitely not Parcheesi. As I've stated, there is a mountain of evidence, scientific and anecdotal, that points to the social and intellectual benefits of chess. Thousands of kids in chess programs all around the country have been transformed by their involvement in the game. I have seen it with the young people I have coached, and I have heard it in all the cities I have visited in my travels. Chess works!

(1) http://www.nycenet.edu/daa/reports/Class%20of%202001_presentation.pdf
(2) http://archives.lincolndailynews.com/2004/Aug/05/Features_new/teaching.shtml
(3) http://www.ed.gov/nclb/overview/welcome/closing/edlite-slide007.htm

One

———

CHESS

IMPACTS

MY

LIFE

The secret to success, happiness, achieving your desires, all of the things that we as humans do and aspire to be, comes down to one concept: the ability to accurately assess your position. Everything you do in life is a move and there will be a response. This is a concept that has been bubbling in my mind and it comes alive for me on the chessboard.

— WILL SMITH, ACTOR

♟ DISCOVERY

I remember the afternoon I first fell in love with chess. I was in the library at Brooklyn Technical High School working on a class project during study-time. Scanning the shelves for some reference material, I noticed a dusty black book with the word *chess* in faded block letters. Curious, I pulled the book down, brushed it off, and opened it. The yellowed pages were filled with multiple diagrams of what I took to be chess setups. Bizarre symbols that seemed like some secret spy code appeared on every page. The accompanying explanations used words that sounded like the language of war, where terms like "maneuver" and "redeployment" seemed to be describing important battle plans. Puzzled and secretly excited by this mysterious discovery, I checked the book out at the front desk. That simple act would seal my fate as an addict of an ancient game that has captivated millions of minds—kings and queens, scientists and philosophers, athletes and actors, grandparents and little kids—for over fourteen hundred years. And it would bring meaning and direction to the disorder that had been my young life.

♟ SACRIFICE

My first experience with the chess concept of sacrifice—giving up something of value in order to attain something more valuable in return—occurred when I was two years old. In 1968, my mother, a single parent desperate for her kids to escape a life of poverty, decided to take advantage of a new U.S. immigration policy that was opening doors to people from all over the Caribbean. Entrusting my brother Devon, sister Alicia, and me to the care of our grandmother (my dad was living in the United States), she traveled to New York City with the hope of finding decent employment. Initially she worked as a live-in nanny taking care of the kids of a well-to-do family on Long Island. Eventually, she moved on to other low-wage positions before finally landing an office job doing clerical work. When she had finally saved up enough money and had secured our visas, she sent for us. The entire process would take ten years.

I took the separation hard. While I made friends easily, not having my mom or dad around left a hole. Our grandmother, Irma Cormack, who we called Mama, filled the gap as best she could. A stern woman who had once been a schoolteacher, she made sure our basic needs were met. Her late-night stories of duppies (ghosts) and obeah men (voodoo priests) kept us both terrified and entertained, her voice crackling with the passion and intensity of someone who had seen such things up close.

From time to time, she would treat us to hot roasted peanuts from the peanut man when he came rolling by with his cart. Having already parented and raised seven children, she was big on discipline and did not hesitate to give us the occasional whipping when we got out of hand. I seemed to bear the brunt of most of the beatings for things like sneaking out of the yard to go see what Devon, older by eight years, was doing with his friends, or for drawing on every single page of a notebook that my mother had sent earlier in the summer for school. Being a sensitive child, I hated being hit for what seemed like normal boyish behavior; many of my tears came from feeling as if my mom might have treated me differently. Though I loved my grandmother, I often fantasized about getting away from Jamaica and living a whole new life.

That day came like a dream.

In 1978, our papers finally went through. On a beautiful sunny day in August, my siblings and I boarded a plane with a few packed belongings and headed for New York. I could not have been more excited. I had spent the past year in a state of near depression, feeling ever more alone and confused. There was very little to satisfy my inquisitive mind and I would read the same comic book nine or ten times to divert myself. Once again, a birthday had passed without toys or books, and I had given up hope that I would one day own a bike. When I had finished third in my class at the prestigious Wolmer's Boys High School,* Mama, noticing my despondency and having nothing to offer in celebration of my achievement, hugged me proudly and stressed the importance of doing one's best for its own sake. I believed her, internalizing that lesson to this day, but I couldn't help but wonder what else life had to offer.

Looking back from the runway, I could see she was beaming with joy and anticipation at the possibilities that life was about to offer the three of us. Her ten years of love, dedication, and hard work were coming to an end; the goal had been reached. On that day, as the plane banked over the mountainside near Kingston and soared north by northwest to the U.S. coastline, I shared her happiness and hopefulness. I did not realize that it was the last time I would see her alive.

♟ LATERAL MOVE

The reunion at John F. Kennedy Airport was exciting and confusing. I had seen my mother four or five times when she had visited home on vacation, but those brief meetings had basically left us strangers. She looked like a younger version of Mama, with the same light skin and

---

*Fifth-graders in Jamaica take a placement exam to try to get into the nation's top schools, of which Wolmer's was one.

straight hair that made her almost close to passing for white. Her eyes mirrored the excitement in Mama's eyes; the decade-long journey for their progeny had been inextricably intertwined. Still, my mother's challenge had been different. Her sacrifice had been one of intimacy, ten years without the subtle joys of watching her children blossom, of missed kisses and hugs, of lost laughter and soft tears, and of not being able to provide the love and security only a mother can give. It would take me a long time, and only after I had my own children, to begin to appreciate the full depth of her loss. Those years had essentially vanished, never to be recaptured. She had given up knowing us, and us knowing her, to secure our futures in the great land of opportunity.

From all the stories I'd heard, living in America was going to be like one big party. The programs on television showed beautiful people with nice clothes, big houses, and fancy cars. Rumor had it that there was a street paved with gold. Before we had left, I had made a twenty-dollar bet with Devon that we would live in a skyscraper with a pool on the roof. He laughed, looked at me to see if I was serious, and then tried to talk me out of it. I insisted. Finally, he shook his head and took the bet.

As we left the airport and drove down Linden Boulevard in Brooklyn, my eyes darted back and forth like a hummingbird. Eager to see mansions and rolling gardens, I was confused by the sights: garbage on the streets, shops smeared with graffiti, gaping potholes in the roads. Abandoned buildings with smashed windows resembling a skull's empty eye sockets seemed to haunt every other corner. I was trying to wrap my mind around this twisted version of America when the car slowed to a stop in front of an old two-story tenement. Devon would later remark that it reminded him of a jailhouse.

As we exited the car, some kids stared at us as though we were naked Aborigines visiting the city for the first time. An ambulance, siren blaring, raced by. Confused by the surreal scene, I asked my mom, "A who we a visit?"

Her answer was sharp and abrupt, her still-thick Jamaican patois sizzling from my unintended insult. "Wha' yu mean? Dis is your home!"

We walked up to the second floor and entered a cramped space that would be the first apartment I had ever set foot in. It had all the basics: a living room, small kitchen, and bathroom. Toward the back were two bedrooms. One was for my mother. The other had two beds, one of which had a rollout underneath. Devon, his eyes crestfallen, noticed the disappointment on my face. "Who need a pool 'pon the roof, anyway?" he said. He never asked me for the twenty bucks.

♟ REPEATING MOVES

Within a couple of weeks, I was trudging off to a new school—Arthur S. Somers Junior High, better known as J.H.S. 252. I was revolted by the graffiti on the outside walls; to mar a school in Jamaica in such a way was like spray-painting the Lincoln Memorial. Since I was an immigrant student, I was given a standard reading test to see which class I should be placed in. The test showed I was reading on a twelfth-grade level, and I was put in 7SP— the top class in the seventh grade.

After the first day, I went home and told my mother that something had to be wrong. The math we had begun to do was math I had been doing in Jamaica at the end of *fifth* grade. Unable to take the day off from work and unsure of exactly how to challenge the system, she told me to take in my report card from the year before. When I returned to school the following day, the guidance counselor looked at it like it was Monopoly money. I'll never forget the look on her face as she insisted that I was in the best class available, that I would be with kids my own age. It's not clear to me now what other decision she should have made, but I felt certain that I did not belong in that class. Her irritated brush-off would have consequences I'm sure she never intended.

It would not take long for my motivation to evaporate as school, once the most challenging part of the day became flat-out boring. I found I could just listen to the teachers during class, and then take the tests and still do well. Math, which had always been my favorite subject, turned into forty minutes of white noise. My math teacher, a short white man with a bushy mustache, tried to challenge us once a month by giving the class a particularly difficult problem. Usually about four or five of us would get it right, upon which we would pile into his car during lunchtime and drive to the neighborhood Burger King for free burgers and fries. I went every time, not because I was smarter than most of my classmates, but because I had seen the math before. I remember at times feeling embarrassed that I could simply glance at the problem and know the answer while the others, who were just learning the material, struggled to figure out the solution. These were the bright kids (we would skip the eighth grade altogether) whose parents valued education. We were being shortchanged from the start without knowing how acutely this would affect our futures.

That a poor country like Jamaica could be that far ahead of the United States in teaching its young was baffling to me then, disgraceful to me now. Over time I would learn that this was not the norm in America, that skin color, the neighborhood one lived in, and low expectations formed a three-headed monster that routinely ate up the potential of millions of kids. My wife, Michele, would later tell me how she had experienced this firsthand, how she had been valedictorian at her junior high in Bushwick, Brooklyn, and had gotten a scholarship to attend high school at the mostly white Friend's Seminary in Manhattan, only to discover that she had been grossly underprepared to compete on equal terms. Thankfully, she is the type of person who attacks challenges; despite the initial embarrassment and resentment, she doggedly made up the gap through dint of effort and hard work. Her bachelor's degree from Columbia and her master's from New York University are a testament to how a bright kid can rise to the occasion, and even excel, once given the opportunity.

For me, after sitting day by day in classes that droned on forever, school slowly went from being the promise of the future to the obligation of the present. Fortunately, there were a few interesting subjects: social studies and the history of the United States were brand new to me, and I also enjoyed listening to my science teacher, a tall burly man with big expressive hands, a round stomach, and a great sense of humor.

Other distractions also kept me preoccupied: I made new friends and I had a huge crush on the prettiest girl in school. I also had the challenge of trying to bridge the culture gap. This was before musical artists like Elephant Man and Sean Paul infused reggae rhythms into hip-hop and r&b, making Jamaican culture cool and sexy. In 1978, having an island accent meant you were one of the *boat people*. Thankfully, I have an ear for languages: I was able to pick up the Brooklyn twang and slang quickly. I learned all about American sports through television, my favorite player at the time being Red Sox–killer Bucky Dent of the New York Yankees. I was far behind the other boys in actually playing the sports themselves, and was invariably one of the last kids picked when it came time to choose sides. Still, the few friends I had treated me well, inviting me over to their houses to hang out and play games. In those two years of junior high, I ended up learning far more outside of school than I did in the classroom.

♟ TRAPS

Life around the neighborhood was like the Wild West. It seemed as if every other day a stray bullet was hitting some kid as drug dealers fought one another over turf. I remember watching from my living room window as two guys shot at each other in broad daylight like it was high noon at the OK Corral. The three kids that they sent scurrying away in terror were the least of their concerns. Getting mugged was hardly a novelty (I was mugged twice), but the consequences of fighting back were often brutal. It was borderline insanity to wear anything fashionable because sooner or later some guy was going to ask if it might not be in your best interest to loan it to him for safekeeping. You might as well have screamed "Pick me, please" if you decided to wear a sheepskin jacket or Adidas sneakers. Guys who tried to do the manly thing and resist got stomped, stabbed, or shot.

The neighborhood seemed to be under constant police surveillance. Groups of young men were randomly pulled over at any time of day and told to spread-eagle. Most searches through school bags and pockets yielded nothing, in which case the boys were told to move along. The running joke, which still applies in almost every Black neighborhood in America, was that you had better watch out because there was an APB (all points bulletin) out on a "young Black man in blue jeans and a jacket."

In that kind of environment, bizarre stuff happened all the time. I remember one evening talking with my best friend, Steffen, in the entranceway to his building when a thug we knew walked up to us and demanded we hand over our jackets. We laughed at first—after all, we spoke to the guy regularly—but when he repeated himself, we realized from the cold look on his face that he was serious.

The worst part was that he was holding the small hand of his two-year-old son, and the kid's eyes seemed blank and unconcerned, as if Daddy took him on raids all the time. Steffen and I glanced at each other nervously. Although it was two of us and only one of him (well two, if you counted the little guy), we knew we didn't stand a chance. While he wasn't tall, he was built like the proverbial fire-plug. He had a square, grisly face that was marred by a small scar on his left cheek. He had been to prison a couple of times, and we knew that he could hurt us, take our jackets, and then nonchalantly go get his kid a hamburger at White Castle. His eyes had a redness that signaled he might have been high on something, and was probably planning to sell our jackets for a few bucks to fill his next prescription.

Knowing all this, we should have stripped our jackets off right away. But we knew the guy *and* his kid was standing right next to him. He even lived upstairs. It was hard to believe it was actually happening. I looked over at Steffen and he reached for his zipper before he put his hands back down. He nervously let out some air as if to say, "This is crazy, man." I shook my head over and over. The moments seemed to crawl by as he stared at us, waiting for his request to be respected. My arms felt watery. A few more seconds passed as we stood our ground.

"That's good," he suddenly grunted. "Never give nobody your shit."

We stood there in stunned silence. He pulled up his coat and showed us a six-inch-long scar snaking across his abdomen. "Some niggaz tried to jump me for my coat, but

I fought them off. One of the suckers cut me. I cold-cocked him across his face. When I finally got my piece, they ran. Too bad I didn't get to pop one." He pulled down his coat. "You young brothers did good. C'mon. Yawl knew I wasn't gonna rob you. My son's right here." Then he turned around, his son in tow, and walked away. We stood motionless until he left, wondering what would have happened if his son had not been with him.

One of the sad things about the neighborhood was that there were so few outlets for the energy of young, restless boys. With no car and, more important, no money, our options were pretty much reduced to playing basketball, touch football, handball, and a few games like dominoes and cards. None of these things required adult supervision, the way a Little League baseball team might. Quite a few of us lived without our fathers at home, so we were pretty much left to our own devices after school and on weekends, when our mothers were just too wiped out from work to monitor our every move.

With nothing to do, we did stuff to amuse ourselves. Some of it was just plain stupid. On one particular occasion, my friend Leon, who would later become one of my chess-playing partners, came up with the idea that we should fake an assault in public. A couple of the guys thought that the idea could be dangerous, but we finally convinced them that it would be harmless fun. I've always been a ham, so I volunteered to be the one who would be the victim. Soon we were all bouncing to Eastern Parkway, the busiest street in the area. When we had almost reached a major intersection, I broke into a sprint with the rest of them loudly giving chase. I raced onto the avenue and faked a fall. My friends leapt on top of me, throwing punches and kicks that must have seemed painful to on-lookers. I lay there for a few seconds as they walked off, and then half-stumbled to my feet. I don't know if I ex-pected applause or what, as people all around stared at me in shock. All of a sudden, four or five men came run-ning up.

"Are you all right?"

"Yes, yes, I'm fine."

"Did you steal something?" I became nervous as one of them started checking my pockets.

"No, no, I didn't."

"Let's go get 'em!" they screamed.

I didn't know what to say as they raced off in the di-rection of my friends. I followed behind slowly, suspecting the worst. When I rounded the corner, I could see the men still running, but there was no sign of my friends. I got to the middle of the block when I heard Leon whis-pering to me from behind a tree inside a park.

"Maurice, are they gone?"

I looked around.

"Yeah, they just turned the corner." All my friends ap-peared from their hiding spots and we ran home laughing.

Another incident could have ended fatally. Leon and I came up with the bright idea of making a sawed-off shot-gun. We sawed off a pair of table legs and then covered it with black tape. Since it wasn't real anyway, we thought that we could just have a little fun scaring some of our friends. The final product was fairly believable, for those who didn't know any better. I knew my mother would kill me if she ever found out, but I excitedly followed along as we snuck up on guys we knew. Most of them laughed when they saw it, and summarily joined in on the fun. We caught one of our friends, also named Maurice, by surprise and he fell to his knees in fear. Another boy, Danté,* got so excited that he pointed it at a passing police car. Luckily the officers didn't notice him or we could have all been in handcuffs, or worse. The full force of the stupidity of the prank smacked us in the face when another friend's brother, unsure who was running up to him, pulled out his very real handgun before realizing that it was just us.

Looking back on these incidents, I can see just how dumb they were. While I make no excuses for this kind of "boys will be boys" behavior, the experience shows what can happen when kids in certain circumstances are left alone for hours on end with nothing constructive to do. The funny thing was that we were the "good" kids. Nothing we did was meant to hurt or steal from anyone. But living under those conditions, there were a few boys I knew who took it further, who felt that the world owed them something. In their minds, the American dream was a fantasy that could only be achieved through illegal means, and with all that free time on their hands, drug dealing and the violence that goes with it seemed like not such a bad way to get there. Slipping into that way of

*Not his real name.

thinking was incredibly easy, especially since the only males in the neighborhood living the glamorous life of fancy clothes, BMWs, and hot women were the drug dealers.

School often felt like a holding cell instead of the haven for learning and personal development that it's supposed to be. Speeches about the hard work needed to get an education and a decent job rang hollow and unconvincing when, in the end, the only Black people we knew who were getting seriously paid were athletes, entertainers, and the aforementioned dealers. Almost twenty-five years later, in poor Black neighborhoods all across America, community leaders still seem to be preaching the same ol' message to a disenchanted, discouraged audience. I was one of the lucky ones: My saving grace came over thirty-two pieces and sixty-four squares.

♟ DEVELOPMENT

On that fateful day when I picked up the book in my high school library, chess burst into my life like spring sunshine following a month of rain. I had been plodding along at Brooklyn Tech—although the curriculum was a real challenge, I did not feel any real motivation to do well. My daily routine had become mundane: wake up, go to school, come home, do homework, hang out with friends, go to bed, and do the same thing all over again the next day. I wasn't one of the in-kids, and I tried and failed to make both the football and baseball team. Trying to find my niche in a school of over four thousand kids proved difficult, and half the time I felt lost and out of place. Not being able to wear stylish clothes and sneakers was still an annoying reality, although most of the kids (boys *and* girls) simply ignored rather than teased. I didn't have a clue where I was heading—that is, until I was bitten by the chess bug.

With the passion of a sinner who had found religion, I pored over any chess paraphernalia I could get my hands on, hoping, with each page, to unearth the deepest mysteries of the game. I pestered my dad (who now lived in New York and who I got to see once a week) to buy me chess books and I studied them with missionary zeal, imprinting on my mind patterns and ideas, subtle strategies and crushing blows for use against future unsuspecting opponents. The many technical terms—isolani, intermezzo, zugzwang, to name a few—became as familiar to me as balls, strikes, and home runs in a baseball game, and I learned to rattle off the names of the greatest players from times past—Emanuel Lasker, Alexander Alekhine, Vasily Smyslov, Bobby Fischer—as easily I could talk about Joe DiMaggio, Hank Aaron, Willie Mays, and the legendary Babe Ruth.

After learning chess notation, a system of letters and numbers that allows players to record each game played, I was able to review some of the grandest moments in chess history: Wilhelm Steinitz vs. Curt von Bardeleben in 1895, where World Champion Steinitz, playing the white pieces, chased Bardeleben's king back and forth the way a cat would a mouse, all the while leaving his own

pieces precariously hovering on a line that divided exis-
tence and nothingness, before his opponent, humiliated
by the endless string of attacks, left the scene without ad-
mitting to the inevitable defeat; José Raúl Capablanca vs.
Frank Marshall in 1918, where Capablanca, facing a ferocious new idea that his opponent had spent years devis-
ing, defended like a master fencer, ducking and parrying
before turning the point on his demoralized adversary; or
Bent Larsen vs. Boris Spassky in 1970, where a black
pawn broke free from its normal plodding life, raced down
the board like Carl Lewis chasing gold at the Olympics,
and broke into the ranks of the white army with devastating effect, a tiny H-bomb creating chaos, despair, and, finally, death.

The games of the grandmasters were artistic, sym-
phonic, exciting, and brutal all rolled into one. While
other teenagers wanted to follow the old commercial and
Be Like Mike (as in Michael Jordan), I wanted to be like
another Mike, Mikhail Tal of Latvia, the greatest tactical
genius who ever lived. His games were bench-clearing
brawls. While many of his contemporaries slowly maneu-
vered for position, trying to induce a slight weakness that
they could massage to slow but sure victory, Tal was consumed by the ever-present compulsion to attack. His
pieces moved like sharks sniffing blood in the water. His
games were thrilling, intoxicating, and vicious, like boxer
Mike Tyson in his prime. While Tal's moves were not
always mathematically accurate (computers have since
shown that he made his share of mistakes), his opponents
would get lost in the hurricane of complex possibilities

and naked aggression. At age twenty-three, his audacious style catapulted him to the very top of world chess, making him the youngest world champion in history.

I would replay his games late into the night, my head swirling from the chaos and brazenness of his moves. I felt as though I were watching the legendary battles of King Arthur: bishops slicing the board like blazing arrows, knights trampling the enemy underfoot, kings being ripped from their castles and dragged to the middle of the village square to face the executioner. I dreamed of playing games like that, Maurice Ashley vs. some-top-Russian, where my best moves would dazzle like jewels before my opponent's eyes and leave grandmasters wondering what genius created such a masterpiece. Through Tal's inspiration, and with the passion of a young man who had found his calling, I eventually decided that I wanted to—had to—one day become an international grandmaster.

That goal altered the course of my life in many fundamental ways. For one, my circle of friends shrank. Unintentionally, I built up a wall against my old acquaintances who had begun swimming in the direction of a strong seductive current, where drugs, money, violence, jail, and, in a few sad instances, death were patiently waiting downstream. The shock of yet another teenage companion being arrested often left me cold and numb; all I could do was shake my head.

My mother, who at the time had no idea what future there could be in chess, appreciated how it kept me out of trouble, knowing that wherever I was, a chessboard or chess book was probably not far away. The friends I kept were mostly chess players, and we spent more Friday nights than I care to count locked in combat until the sun woke us from our spell. Even my choice of girlfriends was limited since most were not interested in playing second fiddle to a board game.

While I lost many friends my age, I gained many more who were older. As I sought out the best players I could find, I would frequent the venerable Marshall and Manhattan Chess Clubs, play in local chess tournaments, and visit nearby parks. It was at the chess tables in Prospect Park, the largest in Brooklyn, where I would meet a group of Black chess players who took the game seriously, men in their twenties and thirties who religiously played chess every day after work and all day on the weekends. Although they played chess for money, they were not hustlers; the money was a way of keeping random pretenders from calling next game on the most competitive tables.

I watched with fascination as George "The Fire Breather" Golden battled William "The Exterminator" Morrison in speed chess, marveling at how hands could dart about with the alacrity and precision of a concert pianist when all the moves of the game had to be played in less than five minutes per side and often in under one second per move.

There were others: Ernest Steve Colding, who loved to sing "I Feel Good" by James Brown when he had you by the throat; Chris Welcome, who would blow cigarette smoke over the board when the game started to turn against him; Herminio Baez, the instigator, who made sure you knew what negative chess-playing rumors were being spread about you, including the ones he himself might have started.

There was also Ronnie Simpson, closest to me in age, who noted my enthusiasm and took me under his wing; our many skirmishes hardened me for international competition in the years ahead. And Willie Johnson, nicknamed Pop because he had a child as a teenager, who spotted my talent early and became like a surrogate father to me, giving me time, advice, and even money whenever he saw I needed a little help.

Only later would I realize their importance to me as role models. They made it cool for me to pursue chess as an intellectual activity, which was not popular in our community. Their enormous respect for book knowledge validated all the time I spent studying. Being Expert-level players and viciously competitive, they provided me with a goal to shoot for. I hungered to get better, if only to beat every last one of them, an impulse they welcomed. The age difference also worked in my favor: The adult male contact that I lacked as a child was no longer an issue. I was growing as a chess player and learning how to be a man, all at the same time.

With chess being such an international game, it sparked in me an interest in world affairs, a desire to travel, and the wish to learn various languages. I would read about chess tournaments in exotic locales and dreamily wonder what the city, country, and people were like. At local chess tournaments I would meet players from Russia, England, Germany, France, Colombia, Nigeria, Brazil, the Dominican Republic, Barbados—literally scores of countries where chess had taken root over the years. I befriended and grew to respect a variety of people—whites, Jews, Latinos, Asians—in a way that was highly unlikely for someone from my background. This was a respect born from a common interest, a shared love for a game that created an instant, enduring connection.

Chess also opened my eyes to the empowering nature of books. If I wanted to explore key variations in the Caro-Khan Defense, practice manifold ways to deliver checkmate, or study the finer nuances of rook endgames, there was always a book to satisfy my need. I would get excited when I read a chapter from a book one day and, soon after, apply what I had learned against one of my friends. Unlike at school, where the information studied promised applicability in some far-off future but often seemed virtually irrelevant, almost every chess book I studied produced quick rewards. I could feel myself getting stronger, more knowledgeable on a daily basis. That instructive quality of books opened my eyes: after that, whenever I had an interest—languages, martial arts, weight lifting—I would invariably search for the best book I could find before physically practicing the thing itself.

Would I have developed these various interests or met the people I did if I had not encountered chess? I can't imagine how, at least not to the degree and variety that I did. The game shaped who I was, bringing direction, purpose, quality, and depth to a life full of uncertainty. My love for the game eventually took me to some of the places of my teenage imagination: the Kremlin in Moscow; the beaches of Bermuda, Hawaii, and St. Martin; Parisian nightclubs; cafes in Amsterdam; Las Vegas casinos; and the Tower of London.

My success as a player and coach allowed me to meet luminaries outside of chess, folks like Will Smith, Bill Cosby, former New York City mayors David Dinkins and Rudy Giuliani, and a host of athletes and other actors who enjoy playing the game. I was humbled to understand some of the profound truths chess can teach to a receptive spirit. And I was blessed to be able to pass them on to kids who grew up the way I did.

Did the game save my life? Those words may be too strong. But chess so informed and influenced everything about my life that I can say, without exaggeration, that I would not be the person I am today had it not been for this ancient game.

Two

—

A

BRIEF

HISTORY

OF

CHESS

*The chessboard is the world, the pieces are the phenom-
ena of the Universe, the rules of the game are what we call
the laws of Nature. The player on the other side is hidden
from us.*

—THOMAS HUXLEY, SCIENTIST

♟ OPENING THEORY

Chess has been a part of my life for twenty-five years, but
its history is very long and varied with an origin steeped in
legend and conjecture. One story, told by the Persian poet
Firdawsi (c. 935–1020) in his epic *Book of Kings,* describes the game as being invented to placate an Indian
queen after the death of one of her two sons. In order to
alleviate her worries that it was his brother who had killed
him, the wise men of the kingdom, according to the tale,
had used those original chess pieces to re-create the battle and prove that her son had died honorably. Thus was
born the term *shah mat,* Persian for checkmate, which
most often translates as "the king is dead." While an interesting tale, this account, and various others, belies the
fact that no one really knows exactly when or how chess
truly began to be played.

That India and Persia should feature in this story will come as a surprise to many Westerners, who often associate chess and its references to kings, queens, knights, and bishops with chivalry and the Middle Ages. However, a mountain of historical evidence places the game's early beginnings in India (though there are those who argue for China), where the game was called *chaturanga*, a Sanskrit term meaning "four members" that referred to the four parts of the Indian army: chariots (rooks), elephants (bishops), cavalry (knights), and infantry (pawns). The Persians would later rename the pieces, removing *raja*, or king, and adding *shah* in its place. This paved the way for the new name of the game in all the major European languages: *Schach* in German, *Shakmati* (checkmate) in Russian, and, *échecs* (for check, an attack on the king) in French, which in turn produced the word *chess* in English.

Given its origins in war, it should come as no surprise that there was no queen in the initial game. Instead, there was a vizier (*firzan* or *firz* in Arabic), the adviser to the king. The voracious all-powerful queen that dominates today's game would not cement herself until approximately the fifteenth century, at a time when European queens often ruled alongside, and even in place of, their male counterparts. But more on that later.

Chess spread across Persia like wildfire. The all-powerful caliphs enjoyed playing games, and chess became featured among the popular pastimes. One tale has it that Caliph Amin of Baghdad (reigned 809–813) bought a female slave for two thousand dinars, in large part because of her skill as a chess player. Caliphs kept resident chess players at their courts, the most famous of which was as-Suli.

Stories and poems written at the time featured chess often and attest to the extent to which the game had seeped into popular culture. A love story between the Muslim prince Sharkan and the Christian princess Abrîza is depicted in the popular *Arabian Nights*. Sharkan, distracted by the princess's beauty, loses the game. It will not be the last time a man claims distraction after being defeated by a woman in chess.

When the dark-skinned Moors brought chess with them during the Arab conquest of Spain, the game took its first toehold in European society. In Iberia, chess was taken up with a passion and zeal that quickly elevated it to the "royal game." Soon it was being played in all the courts of Europe, where it was considered a necessary part of proper regal upbringing. Not so clear was how much chess was being played by the masses, since they often worked long hours in service of the royals and had little time for many leisure activities. But from the courts of Charlemagne, the popular French king and Holy Roman Emperor, to the palace of Eleanor of Aquitaine, chess took its place alongside poetry, dancing, horseback riding, and archery as a standard form of royal entertainment.

♟ BAD BISHOP

Despite, and maybe because of, its popularity, chess playing often clashed with the clergy. Although the Koran does not expressly forbid it, some imans saw the game as a distraction, and a promotion of idolatry (there is text in the Koran that restricts the use of images representing animals or people). In Christendom, the game was considered on a par with gambling by some religious leaders. This was due in part to one popular variant of the game in which players threw dice to see what piece to move, thereby making the result based more on chance than on skill. Apparently it had also become a little too popular among a clergy that was supposed to be out preaching the ministry.

Influential Jewish leaders also felt it necessary to ban chess, again because of the gambling connection. Once the game took on its more current form—around the 1500s—however, chess became an acceptable pastime, even on the Sabbath.

Still, the perception of chess as a gambler's game caused problems elsewhere. As recently as 1981, chess was banned in Iran because of the belief that it encouraged gambling. It took a 1988 decree from the Ayatollah Khomeini to deem chess once again acceptable, as long as it was not being played for stakes. He even admitted that it had redeeming intellectual and educational values. This did not stop the Taliban rulers in Afghanistan from later banning chess, throwing participants in jail, and burning the chess pieces. Once the Taliban were ousted from power in 2001 by the U.S. Army for their role in the 9/11 attacks, the people of Afghanistan unearthed their chess sets once again.

♟ PROMOTION

Back in the Middle Ages, exotic chess sets were considered a status symbol in the homes of those who could afford them. The period saw many exquisitely carved masterpieces. The most famous were the Lewis chessmen, which sits today in the British Museum. Discovered in 1831 on the Isle of Lewis, off the western coast of Scotland, the pieces show the solemn expression of an army ready for war. This stood in dramatic contrast to the abstract pieces the Arabs played with, in respect to their prohibition against idolatry. The Charlemagne chess set, apparently made to honor a real battle between a Norman warlord and a Byzantium emperor, is another popular set from the period. It features elephants (today's bishops) and chariots (today's rooks) as well as an actual queen, which showed the early beginnings of chess's transition from a representation of battle to one based on the feudal structure of society.

The late 1400s and early 1500s saw the most dramatic changes in the game's rules. The bishop, who once could only move three squares diagonally (including its own), now was able to fly the length of the board. The pawns were able to move two squares on their first move instead of just one. But the most drastic change of all pertained to the movement of the queen, who went from being able to go only one square at a time diagonally to the unlimited multidirectional monster it is today. In Marilyn Yalom's provocative new book *The Birth of the Chess Queen,* she argues that this acceleration of the queen's power was consistent with the rise of actual queens all over Europe, most notably Spain's Queen Isabelle, who, along with her husband, King Ferdinand, sponsored the voyage of Christopher Columbus. She also draws a connection to the Virgin Mary, who was the subject of quite a few chess carvings, and the cult of love, which saw the elevation of women as romantic figures deserving of courtship and personal sacrifice.

While the reasons may be unclear, the metamorphosis of the queen from the impotent vizier to super-Amazon had rippling effects that changed the game dramatically. For one, the slow strategic game that could have lasted a day or two now could literally end in two moves. This meant that the leisurely game that could be sipped like fine wine became far more frenzied. Players had to concentrate like never before since *la Dame enrageé* (the mad queen) might pounce at any moment and gobble up a few pieces on her way to delivering a swift checkmate. The opening moves took on more importance as one bad move might spell early disaster. Books on the openings systematized the best practices of the times and were necessary reading to anyone who wanted to survive in the early goings. Also, as suggested by Yalom, the speeding up of the game and the rise of competitions may have inadvertently led to a lessening of female involvement. For one, the quickening of the game returned it to its martial roots— games that may have been a cover for romantic encounters now contained a ferocity that was inappropriate for the purpose. While this seems a bit of a stretch, one can imagine that the royals who were trained to play by traveling professionals were also well versed as to how to win quickly if the opportunity presented itself, making the game faster, more competitive, and less romantically engaging. Simultaneously, formal competitions effectively barred women from playing against men, a social convention that is still in effect in many chess circles around the world. (This will be discussed at length in a later chapter.)

Still, there is no question that the new rules served to heighten the overall popularity of the game. Famous chess players toured Europe and visited royal courts. In 1549, Paoli Boi of Italy gained prominence by playing and defeating Pope Paul III. In 1561, the Spanish priest Ruy Lopez wrote a famous treatise that has immortalized him in chess circles. In 1613, chess appeared onstage when Miranda plays against Ferdinand in Shakespeare's *The Tempest*. The royals propagated the new game with zeal: King Charles I of England and Louis XIII of France were considered virtual addicts; the Shah Jahan, who financed the construction of the world-famous Taj Mahal, also had a chess palace built; and Ivan the Terrible of Russia is reputed to have died while about to begin a chess game.

More significantly, the rise of the European middle class, full of desire to emulate their wealthy counterparts, led to a chess explosion on the continent. This also led to the pieces becoming affordable and less ornate. Since many more games were being played, it didn't make sense for the finest masterpieces to be used over and over again. By the 1700s, chess sets of common design overtook the more elegant.

It wouldn't be long before chess gained a foothold in the newly formed United States. As is to be expected, many of the Founding Fathers were keen players. George Washington had a set made of ivory that is now housed in the U.S. National Museum in Washington, D.C. Thomas Jefferson, third president and author of the Declaration of Independence, was also an avid player. He owned several chess sets and, not surprisingly, loved to read famous books on the game. His vice president Aaron Burr was also an enthusiastic player, and they apparently played together. Thus began a long line of executives who played chess, including James Madison, John Quincy Adams, Abraham Lincoln, Theodore Roosevelt, Woodrow Wilson, Jimmy Carter, and Bill Clinton.

Maybe the most famous and fervent American statesman who played chess was Benjamin Franklin. Though he had many skills as a printer, author, and scientist, chess held a special place in his heart. A measure of his skill was the fact that Jefferson bragged that he was just as good a player as his friend Franklin. (Presidential ego is something.) Jefferson also wrote that the reason Franklin was so popular in France was because he played chess with beautiful and powerful women. Franklin penned the first chess article published in the United States and titled it "The Morals of Chess." It shows his passion and respect for the game from the very beginning: "The Game of Chess is not merely an idle amusement; several very valuable qualities of the mind, useful in the course of human life, are to be acquired and strengthened by it, so as to become habits ready on all occasions; for life is a kind of Chess, in which we have often points to gain, and competitors or adversaries to contend with, and in which there is a vast variety of good and ill events, that are, in some degree, the effect of prudence, or the want of it. . . ."

He goes on to mention a number of qualities one derives from playing the game: foresight, circumspection, caution, and an optimistic outlook. His spends the rest of the article dealing with issues of sportsmanship. In one section, speaking in an era before the prevalence of chess clocks dramatically sped up each game, he warns against impatient behavior.

> If your adversary is long in playing, you ought not to hurry him, or express any uneasiness at his delay; not even by looking at your watch, or taking up a book to read: you should not sing, nor whistle, nor make a tapping with your feet on the floor, or with your fingers on the table, nor do anything that may distract his attention: for all these displease, and they do not prove your skill in playing, but your craftiness and your rudeness.

It sounds like this must have happened to him a few times. In another section, he addresses the recently popular habit of trash-talking: *"You must not, when you have gained a victory, use any triumphing or insulting expressions, nor show too much of the pleasure you feel. . . ."*

Tell that to the chess hustlers at Washington Square Park in New York City. Still, despite the quaintness of some of his dictums, they are still pretty much in use today by professional players.

During Franklin's time, the best player in the world was a Frenchman by the name of André Philidor. His book, *The Analysis of Chess,* was a best seller and he would stun onlookers by playing three games at a time while blindfolded (with players relaying the moves to him orally). He was also a composer of over twenty operas, but his most enduring claim is a quote of his that some say presaged the revolutionary movements of the eighteenth century: "The pawns are the soul of chess." Shortly after that, the royalty in France would be overturned and beheaded by the peasants in yet another instance of life mirroring chess and vice versa.

In the nineteenth century, with worldwide expansion continuing at a furious pace, chess tournaments began to increase. Europe remained the center of chess development, with the English and French as the leading players (as they were in world politics). In the middle of the century, however, an American genius named Paul Morphy foreshadowed future Yankee ingenuity by defeating all the top European players save the Englishman Howard Staunton, who seemed to be avoiding him. Morphy would become, according to the *Oxford Encyclopedia of Chess,* the first American to be acknowledged the best in the world at a specialized field. Sadly, his career was short-lived (1861–1863), and his life took a turn for the worse when he was stricken by bouts of paranoia and self-talk. Though he wrote no books, his games showed a daring and logic that was far ahead of his time.

♟ TRANSITION

The great democratization of chess began in the twentieth century. No longer was it considered a game for the upper crust of society. Inexpensive chess sets found their way into the homes of the average citizen in virtually every country. Tournaments became more and more routine, and the best players traveled far and wide to compete in the top events. After World War II, the International Chess Federation (Fédération Internationale des Échecs, or FIDE) was formed to organize the world championships and coordinate world chess.

This marked the official beginning of a new chess power as the Soviet players, aided by government support and systematized training, gained a stranglehold on high-level play. This had been brewing for decades before the war, first by the Bolsheviks, who had toppled the old tsarist government in the 1917 revolution and promoted chess as a means to build character and mental acuity among the vast peasant population. The ensuing Communist regime, headed primarily by Stalin, saw chess as one measure of their superiority over the West, and even created a five-year plan to create the best competitors in the world. Top chess players were treated like professional sportsmen, receiving substantial stipends and traveling abroad frequently in an age when the Iron Curtain kept most of its citizens firmly locked in.

Chess quickly became a Russian national pastime, on a par with soccer and ice hockey. Young "pioneer" clubs tutored kids as young as four years old; super-talented youngsters would be singled out for special training in a manner similar to future generations of young figure skaters and gymnasts. Each one was expected to be the ideal socialist, supporting the system that had created them by crushing the Western players. Alexander Ilyin-Zhenevsky, chief commissar of the General Reservists' Organization in Moscow, stated it firmly: "Chess cannot be apolitical as in capitalist countries."* Those who failed to perform would suddenly find their valuable travel privileges suspended indefinitely, and one of their many stipend-hungry comrades quickly filling their place.

While other countries produced stars of note, none were able to rival the Soviet avalanche that saw one chess assassin replace another in turn—that is, until the advent of a paradoxical chess genius from Brooklyn named Bobby Fischer.

His love for chess was total, and even fellow grandmasters were stunned by his almost pathological obsession with the game. He was never without a pocket chess set, and if a conversation turned to more worldly topics, he had no problem whipping it out and ignoring the speaker. In

*From *Bobby Fischer Goes to War,* by David Edmonds and John Eidinow.

1956, at the tender age of thirteen, he played a game of such magnificence that it would be dubbed "The Game of the Century," and at fifteen he would become the youngest grandmaster in the history of the game. For him, chess was life. He wanted nothing more than to make his rivals "squirm." On one occasion he said, "Chess is like war over the board. The object is to crush the opponent's mind." And at another time: "I like the moment when I break a man's ego."

Naturally, the Soviets were fascinated by him. While they deplored his limited, almost childlike approach to the world outside of chess, they were profoundly impressed by his obvious genius for *their* game. His brilliance caught their attention very early on, and they quietly became obsessed by him, keeping files of his games and analyzing them for any weakness. While this was done with all the strong Western players, Fischer was an animal of a different breed against whom they felt they had to be meticulously prepared. At round-robin tournaments (where each participant plays all the others in the tournament), Fischer claimed that the top Soviets would make early draws with each other, saving energy for their games against him. Fischer noted this with special disgust. "There was open collusion between the Russian chess players. They agreed ahead of time to draw the games they played against each other. Every time they drew they gave each other a half a point."

Later, world championship candidate and Soviet defector Victor Korchnoi argued that this was not done just to Fischer, that he, too, had been a victim of this process.

While these claims remain unconfirmed, recently revealed papers seem to suggest that Fischer and Korchnoi were not just spouting invectives after a loss.

It all came to a head when, in 1971, Fischer stormed through the candidates' matches (a series of games designed to produce a challenger to the World Champion) by crushing his world-class opponents with unprecedented dominance. First, it was the Soviet grandmaster Mark Taimanov who went down in ignominious defeat after losing an unbelievable six games in a row. Fischer then dispatched the Danish grandmaster Bent Larsen by the same astonishing score before bringing down another Soviet, former world champion Tigran Petrosian. Then, in the summer of 1972, with the whole world watching, Fischer defeated the reigning World Champion Boris Spassky by a final score of six games to two. The image of a lone American crushing what seemed like the entire Soviet chess establishment at the height of the Cold War captivated a viewing public that cared nothing about chess per se. Before the match, the *Washington Post* had written: "A Fischer victory would strike at the basic claim of Soviet ideology." After his victory, Fischer himself was fired up enough to say, "It's given me great pleasure as a free person to have smashed this thing."

In the United States, Fischer was treated like an Olympian. National Security adviser Henry Kissinger called to congratulate him, and he made the cover of the major magazines. Women wrote him love letters. (This is a chess player we're talking about!) Unfortunately, when he could have cemented his reputation as a great American hero, Fischer's paranoia and general hatred for the Soviet government led him to seemingly self-destruct. He complained that the Soviet secret police were out to kill him, and he refused to defend his title without total compliance to his demands. During the 1974 cycle of the world championships, FIDE decided that he was being unreasonable and awarded the crown to the next deserving qualifier in line, Anatoly Karpov of Russia.

Fischer went into seclusion for almost twenty years before returning to play another controversial match against his old rival Spassky in war-torn Yugoslavia. This was at a time when Americans were not allowed to do business in the country, an issue Fischer further compounded by spitting on a U.S. State Department document in the presence of scores of members of the media. Fearing arrest on his return to the country, Fischer avoided the United States for more than a decade, traveling to various countries before settling in Japan, where he was recently arrested for carrying an invalid passport. As of this writing, he is facing extradition back to the United States. (The Icelandic government has since issued him a passport to their country.) While he still has his fans, he has managed to alienate many people with his anti-American and anti-Semitic views. While Fischer "the man" seems to harbor a slew of significant personal weaknesses, many chess players prefer to remember him for his dynamic exploits over the chessboard that prove, in some minds at least, that he was the greatest chess player who ever lived.

♟ OPEN GAME

The post-Fischer era saw chess blossom like never before. Membership in the U.S. Chess Federation (USCF) quintupled in the few years following the match, and a crop of U.S. grandmasters seemed to mushroom overnight. World championship matches became million-dollar affairs, and open chess tournaments saw significant increases in their prize funds. In the late 1980s, scholastic chess in the United States began its major rise, reaching a high point in 1991 with the victory of the Raging Rooks, a team I coached. The media sensation that accompanied a team from Harlem winning a national chess championship, and the continued support for children's chess by various organizations, caused yet another spike in USCF membership.

The late eighties and nineties saw chess's broadening appeal challenge some long-held myths. First, Judit Polgar, one of three chess-playing sisters from Hungary, broke Bobby Fischer's thirty-year record and became the youngest grandmaster of all time at the age of fifteen years, four months, and twenty-eight days (Fischer's record was fifteen years, six months, and one day). Leaving many male victims in her wake, she won several tournaments that had previously been dominated by men and broke into the ranks of the top ten players in the world. Her accomplishments have helped to usher in a new age of women's chess around the globe, where women from

China to the Ukraine have followed her example to dramatically raise the game to a new level of excellence.

Another myth to be shattered was the belief, held by many top grandmasters, that a machine could never bridge the gap between silicon and human thought. In 1997, Deep Blue, a chess-playing computer designed by programmers at IBM, shocked the world of chess by defeating the reigning World Champion and highest ranking player of all time, Garry Kasparov, in a match that had entranced millions of curious onlookers. Though many tried to build up this Man vs. Machine match as a potential proving ground for the superiority of artificial intelligence, the human's loss, though humbling, merely showed how far computers had come at playing a game as amenable to brute force calculation as chess.

The computer's victory, however, did fundamentally change how chess professionals prepare for contests, as grandmasters now consistently practice and conduct research with the latest versions of chess-playing computer software. More recent matches between humans and computers have resulted in draws, leaving the jury still out on which entity truly plays better chess.

In 1999, another chess stereotype bit the dust when a black man, your present author, became the first in history to attain the title of International Grandmaster. My achievement had an electrifying effect in the world of chess (both Black and non-Black) and with those who doubted the intellectual capabilities of African Americans, including some African Americans themselves.

After fourteen hundred years, chess seems to be truly arriving. While television coverage of major matches is still in its infancy, the game has exploded in popularity over the Internet. Yahoo and America Online count chess among their most popular games, and other chess Web sites routinely see players from around the world check in day or night to get a game. Talented kids in remote rural areas who own a computer can now find regular competition, and chess-playing computer software has accelerated the growth of prodigies to such an extent that the youngest grandmaster is now only twelve years old! Brand-new events with previously unheard of prizes promise to take chess in the direction of other well-established individual sports such as golf and tennis. With all these factors driving it forward, chess seems poised to flourish at a much higher level in the twenty-first century.

Three

THINKING

AND

CHESS

Stats and Studies

Via the squares on the chessboard, the Indians explain the movement of time and the age, the higher influences which control the world and the ties which link chess and the human soul.

—AL-MASUDI, ARAB EXPLORER

Over the centuries, it has become commonplace among fans of chess to insist that the game has intellectual benefits far beyond the sixty-four squares. It was only a matter of time before researchers turned their attention to the topic in an attempt to definitively answer the question "What effect does playing chess have on the mind?"

The initial studies focused on professionals, beginning with renowned psychologist Alfred Binet's 1893 study of memory using blindfolded chess players. Later, noted psychologist and chess master Adriaan de Groot did a far more comprehensive study of what differentiates top chess players from less accomplished ones. While the results proved fascinating to anyone interested in chess psychology, they had little value in the broader intellectual and educational community.

The first study of note to focus on chess and aptitude in young people was conducted during the 1973–74 school year by Dr. Albert Frank at the Lisanga School in Kisangani, Zaire. Taking a group of ninety-two students between the ages of sixteen and eighteen from a fourth-year humanities class, Dr. Frank randomly split the group in half (experimental and control) and gave them a battery of aptitude tests. The experimental group was then taught chess for two hours each week with optional play after school and during vacations.

The results were surprising. After only one year of chess study, the students participating in the chess course showed a marked improvement on their numerical and verbal aptitudes. This held true not only for the better chess players, but for the chess group as a whole. The increase in verbal ability proved most puzzling to the authors of the study, as they were unable to provide an adequate explanation as to why chess should influence the development of verbal skills.

Another experiment was conducted during the 1974–76 school years by Johan Christiaen at the Assenede Municipal School in Gent, Belgium. Forty fifth-grade students were split randomly into two groups and tested, the most important being Piaget's tests for cognitive development. The experimental group received forty-two one-hour chess lessons using the textbook *Jeugdschaak* (Chess for Youths).

When the kids were retested at the end of sixth grade,

those who had taken chess were significantly ahead in intellectual maturation of their non-chess-playing counterparts. The transition from Piaget's *concrete* level (stage three) to his *formal* level (stage four), where children begin deducing and hypothesizing by using more complex logic and judgment, was far accelerated in the chess-playing kids. The study's dramatic findings compelled many scientists to call for other studies to confirm and broaden the results. The hunt was on.

The first important follow-up study was conducted over a four-year period by Dr. Robert Ferguson using mentally gifted seventh- through ninth-grade students from the Bradford Area School District in Bradford, Pennsylvania. The project, carried out from 1979 to 1983, was federally funded during the first three years and locally supported in the final year. A pretest was conducted on the students to determine their levels in two key areas: critical thinking and creativity. The students were asked to choose their own interests; fifteen chose chess, while the rest chose various other activities, including computers. Each group met once a week for thirty-two weeks; in total, each group spent sixty to sixty-four hours on their preferred activity.

As in the previous studies, the chess group significantly outperformed the non-chess groups on the posttests, not just once, but for four years in a row. While the increase in critical thinking had been expected, it was the striking difference in three areas of creativity—fluency, flexibility, and, in particular, originality—that was most remarkable. While exciting, the limited student sampling (fifteen) and the already high performance level of the children left even the experimenter seeking broader confirmation.

It wasn't long in coming. In 1984, the International Chess Federation (FIDE) reported the results of a project conducted in Venezuela by the Ministry for the Development of Intelligence that included 4,226 second-grade students. The experiment showed an increase of intelligence quotient (IQ) in both male and female students as well as across all socioeconomic levels. Upon seeing the results, celebrated behavioral psychologist B. F. Skinner wrote, "There is no doubt that this project in its total form will be considered as one of the greatest social experiments of this century."

The study had a far-reaching effect. FIDE reported a huge increase in worldwide scholastic chess, with as many as thirty countries implementing chess in the curriculum of thousands of schools. A Canadian study in 1992 confirmed the Venezuelan findings when a group of first-grade chess students significantly outperformed their peers in math, both in problem solving and comprehension. In addition, young students taking part in a two-year chess study in Moldavia showed marked improvement in memory, organizational skills, fantasy, and imagination, according to the country's Education Ministry.

These approaches caught the eye of educators in the United States, who were looking for a solution to one of the most recalcitrant problems of the time: how to properly teach and motivate inner-city kids in school. In 1986, the American Chess Foundation (ACF, later renamed

Chess in Schools), under the leadership of the late philanthropist Faneuil Adams Jr., began sending chess instructors into various public schools throughout New York
City. The success of the program in the first five years, especially after one of the schools won a National Chess
Championship, prompted the ACF to commission a study
under the authorship of Dr. Stuart Margulies. Consider-
ing the emphasis placed on reading scores, the ACF decided to revisit the Zaire results by studying what effect
playing chess might have on literacy in its student population.

Fifty-three elementary students in the chess program
from Roberto Clemente Elementary School in the Bronx,
New York, were tested and their results compared to a
control group of 1,118 nonparticipants. The outcome was
a watershed moment in chess education: The chess students showed such considerable gains that even the author of the study was surprised.

This surprise, however, was not shared by Felton M.
Johnson, superintendent of Community School District
Nine in New York City. "I am particularly pleased by Dr.
Stuart Margulies' study," he said. "I am not surprised by
the significant improvement in reading scores achieved by
our students. Inherent in any demonstrated learning is a
mental discipline that channels knowledge and concepts
in such a way that they ensure meaningful learning. A
good chess player must demonstrate a variety of higher order thinking skills that are transferable directly to virtually
any academic discipline."

The study sent a strong ripple through those paying attention in the field of education. As stories of inner-city youth winning major scholastic chess championships started making the daily newspapers, watchful principals began lining up to get their kids involved in chess programs. Scholastic chess teams sprung up overnight; winning programs found themselves being invited to City Hall to receive mayoral citations. The New York City Schools Chess Program exploded to tens of thousands of kids within the next several years, and chess began to blossom in schools all across the country.

In 1999, Dr. Marguiles and colleague Dr. Kathleen Speeth, supported by Chess in Schools, created an original study to test the effect of chess instruction on emotional intelligence, the importance of which has long been championed by multiple intelligence theorist Howard Gardner as critical to success in the classroom. The factors assessed were self-confidence, empathic respect for others, mood management, frustration tolerance, and sustained efforts to achieve personal goals. The remarks of an experimental group of sixty fifth-grade students, evenly split between boys and girls, and a control group of the same composition were evaluated by three independent scorers. The results were off the scale. In every single category, the chess-playing students, with 91.4 percent of their responses being scored as emotionally intelligent, outstripped the non-chess-playing ones, who scored 64.4 percent overall. Intriguingly, the greatest differentiator was on the topic of respect for others: The chess students showed a whopping 42 percent difference in their scores.

These results have been borne out in schools. Educators at Roberto Clemente report that chess has improved not only academic scores but social performance as well. "The effects have been remarkable," says one teacher. "Not only have the reading and math skills of these children soared, their ability to socialize has increased substantially, too. Our studies have shown that incidents of suspension and outside altercations have decreased by at least 60 percent since these children became interested in chess."

"I like the aspect of socialization," says Jerome Fishman, a guidance counselor at J.H.S. 231 in Queens, New York. "You get into friendly, competitive activity where no one gets hurt. It's strategic, and you use logic to plan an attack. . . . Aside from being good for the cognitive development of these youngsters, chess develops their social skills, too. It makes them feel [as if] they belong. Whenever we get a child transferred from another school who may have maladaptive behavior, our principal [Dr. Wilton Anderson] suggests chess as a way of helping him find his niche."

Other less stringent studies and thousands of individual stories have borne out the conclusions of these studies. Connie Wingate, principal of P.S. 123 in New York, may have said it best: "This is wonderful! This is marvelous! This is stupendous! It's the finest thing that ever happened to this school. . . . It has been an absolute plus for the students who were directly involved as well as for the rest of the school. . . . More than anything else, chess makes a difference . . . what it has done for these children is simply beyond anything that I can describe." With such an enormous body of empirical and anecdoctal support, it's easy to see why many educators around the country have embraced chess as a primary enrichment activity for their students.

Flow

Could we look into the head of a chess player, we should see there a whole world of feelings, images, ideas, emotion and passion.

—ALFRED BINET, PSYCHOLOGIST

Chess, like love, like music, has the power to make men happy.

—SIEGBERT TARRASCH, GRANDMASTER

What is it about the game of chess that hooks kids and adults? Ask a group of chess players this question and the answers will vary from the game's qualities (complexity, geometric beauty, lack of repetitiveness) to the feelings one experiences while playing (excitement, enjoyment, happiness). No doubt all of these answers, though a bit generalized, are correct. However, recent studies have shed even greater clarity on the reasons for the satisfaction that chess players get from a well-played game. These findings, which show that the feelings are not at all unique to chess, offer a compelling explanation that could have parents and educators rethinking how they motivate young people. In a word, it's all about "flow."

The most famous proponent of flow theory is Professor Mihaly Csikszentmihalyi of the University of Chicago. A psychologist who has devoted much of his life to investigating what makes people "happy," Csikszentmihalyi has written two books, *Flow* and *Finding Flow,* which detail the results of the work of his research team. After interviewing thousands of respondents from around the globe using a method he calls Experience Sampling, he has concluded that people who enjoy life to the fullest are not after happiness per se, but rather optimal experience, or flow. In *Finding Flow,* he explains use of the term: "The metaphor of 'flow' is one that many people have used to describe the sense of effortless action they feel in moments that stand out best in their lives. Athletes refer to it as 'being in the zone,' religious mystics as being in 'ecstasy,' artists and musicians as aesthetic rapture."

What sorts of activities induce flow? According to the professor, those in which the goals are perfectly clear and the responses more or less preset. The key is for the practitioner to be able to use his or her set of skills to meet the challenges as they arise moment to moment. He further notes: "[I]t is easy to enter flow in games such as *chess* [emphasis added], tennis, or poker, because they have goals and rules for action that make it possible for the player to act without questioning what should be done, and how. For the duration of the game the player lives in a self-contained universe where everything is black and white. The same clarity of goals is present if you perform a religious ritual, play a musical piece, weave a rug, write a computer game, climb a mountain, or perform surgery."

Why is flow so important? Dr. Csikszentmihalyi argues that it brings about a state that humans constantly seek: order to consciousness. Most of our waking hours are spent flitting and fleeing from one thing to the next, our thoughts a chaotic jumble that never seem to be able to settle on one subject for very long. This condition, which he calls "psychic entropy," is responsible for much of the boredom we feel when we have nothing particularly challenging to do. In the West, the most frequent way of managing psychic entropy is by watching television, an activity that now consumes an average of five to six hours of a child's day. However, due to the passive nature of the involvement, watching television only rarely contributes to the psychological growth of the individual as it mainly offers titillating entertainment instead of meaningful enlightenment. While its mock scenarios may require attention, watching television is a poor way of developing the ability to be more *attentive*. Frequent channel surfing and the simultaneous viewing of two or more programs is further proof that little concentration is really needed to enjoy the experience.

The ideal state, according to Dr. Csikszentmihalyi, is one of "psychic negentropy," in which all our random thoughts become organized around an activity while our attention becomes fully invested. These activities place such a demand on psychic energy that the slightest distraction might upset the balance. The focus is so complete that the sense of time is distorted: Hours seem to pass by in minutes. My longest chess game, an eight-hour marathon against Grandmaster Dmitri Gurevich in New York in 1988, lasted until two in the morning. After I had lost, I looked around and saw that besides one or two spectators, we were the only players left in the hall. So complete was my concentration on the twists and turns of the battle that food and sleep had become irrelevant. Eight hours might as well have been eight minutes.

Dr. Csikszentmihalyi lists eight major components of flow:

1. The experience usually occurs when we confront tasks we have a chance of completing.
2. We must be able to concentrate on what we are doing.
3. The task undertaken has clear goals.
4. The task undertaken provides immediate feedback.
5. One acts with a deep but effortless involvement that removes from awareness the worries and frustrations of everyday life.
6. The enjoyable experience allows people to exercise a sense of control over their actions.
7. Concern for the self disappears, yet paradoxically the sense of self emerges stronger after the flow experience is over.
8. The sense of the duration of time is altered— hours pass by in minutes, and minutes can stretch out to seem like hours.

All the above points perfectly describe the joys of chess playing. While studies have shown that chess improves concentration, this explanation argues that it may do so because it so easily *induces* concentration. Because the goal in chess is crystal clear (checkmate the enemy king), the feedback continuous (one can see if one is approaching the goal or not), and the sense of control apparent (the player is fully responsible for each and every move), it is easy to become immersed in the activity. Many parents have expressed amazement at seeing a young child who may have been bouncing off the walls suddenly calm down to focus on playing a chess game. More than one visitor has been shocked to witness the total silence and concentration that permeates the hall of a National Scholastic Championship. It is as though the kids have entered into a trance, not the mindless one that comes from incessant TV viewing, but the stimulating yet total involvement that comes from being engrossed in a challenge.

Naturally, I have experienced this feeling countless times since it happens almost every time I pick up a chess piece. One especially memorable moment occurred when I was playing against Grandmaster Robert Kempinski of Poland at a tournament in the lovely German spa town of Bad Wiessee. I had won my first five games of the event and was tied for first going into this critical encounter. My focus on the game, for obvious reasons, was total, but it was one particular instant that stands out. I had outmaneuvered my opponent in the first several moves and, on move seventeen, was contemplating what I should do next.

Suddenly, as though someone had grabbed my hand, I picked up my queen's knight and placed it on a square where it could be captured by one of my opponent's pawns. It was not a terribly unusual sacrifice; it was the type of play that one often sees in various circumstances in that particular opening. But what surprised me was the casual way in which I executed the move, giving away a piece without any real deep calculation and playing the move without a hiccup of uncertainty. The knight just seemed to leap out of my fingers onto the square, as if it knew that its sacrifice would not be in vain, that through its well-timed demise the remaining forces would expand in power, scope, and deadliness. The effect of the move was devastating, as it opened up a breach to the enemy king that my pieces eagerly rushed to fill. Many moves later, after my opponent's king had been harried from the safety of the back row to the dangerous hustle and bustle of the middle of the chessboard, I surrounded it, and delivered checkmate. After the game, I had the unusually pleasant feeling that it was my pieces that had done all the work, that I was but a willing instrument taking them from one square to the next. I had been living in Csikszentmihalyi's self-contained universe of black and white, at one with the pieces in the way a violinist might be at one with a Mozart concerto. I had not even realized that onlookers had completely surrounded our board, so enthralled was I by the intensity of the struggle.

I left the scene in a state of euphoria, not just because

I had won, but mainly because I had experienced every sportsman's dream: to become so completely involved in one's chosen activity that, for the time being, nothing else mattered. For a delicious window in time, it was just me and the game.

I could not have had this amazing experience if I had not felt up to the task. Flow does not happen unless there is a strong correlation between the challenges one faces and the skills one has developed to meet that challenge. If the challenges are too easy, then we will quickly become bored, but if they are too hard, then we will just as easily become frustrated. That is one of the reasons why it is critical for kids to play with other kids or with players of their level of ability. Chess tournaments, with their very accurate ranking (in chess parlance, rating) system, provide a close to precise gauge of the relative strength of the competitors, making it easy for each child to be in an ideally challenging situation. Thus the likelihood that the child will experience flow is increased and the subsequent enjoyment and growth heightened.

Still, does chess, as Tarrasch's quote affirms, have the power to make us happy? Not while we are doing it, according to Dr. Csikszentmihalyi. He argues that "[i]t is the full involvement of flow, rather than happiness, that makes for excellence in life. . . . If a rock climber takes time to feel happy while negotiating a difficult move, he might fall to the bottom of the mountain. The surgeon can't afford to feel happy during a demanding operation, or a musician while playing a challenging score. Only after the task is completed do we have the leisure to look back on what has happened, and then we are flooded with gratitude for the excellence of that experience—then, in retrospect, we are happy."

Which in my book is a long way of saying, yes, chess does have the power to make us happy. With the steps delineated by Dr. Csikszentmihalyi, parents and educators should find it easier to frame interesting solutions to keeping young people motivated year-round in chess, as well as in other engaging pursuits.

Chess and the 40 Developmental Assets™

You sit at the board and suddenly your heart leaps. Your hand trembles to pick up the piece and move it. But what chess teaches you is that you must sit there calmly and think about whether it's really a good idea and whether there are other, better ideas.

—STANLEY KUBRICK, DIRECTOR

More recently, another method of measurement has emerged that further illustrates the potential efficacy of chess as an educational tool. In 1997, the Minneapolis-based Search Institute, an independent nonprofit organization whose mission is to provide leadership, knowledge, and resources to promote healthy children, youth, and communities, identified a framework that has begun to gain currency nationwide. These forty "developmental assets," divided into internal and external assets, have been found by the Institute to be effective predictors of healthy growth in young people. When present, particularly when the number of assets stand at thirty-one or more, the young person is far less likely to engage in high-risk behaviors. In addition, young people who report a greater number of assets also report higher incidences of positive behaviors, such as school success, exhibition of leadership ability, and valuing diversity.

40 DEVELOPMENTAL ASSETS™

Search Institute℠ has identified the following building blocks of healthy development that help young people grow up healthy, caring, and responsible.

Asset Name & Definition

1. **Family support**—Family life provides high levels of love and support.
2. **Positive family communication**—Young person and her or his parent(s) communicate positively, and young person is willing to seek advice and counsel from parent(s).
3. **Other adult relationships**—Young person receives support from three or more nonparent adults.

4. **Caring neighborhood**—Young person experiences caring neighbors.

5. **Caring school climate**—School provides a caring, encouraging environment.

6. **Parent involvement**—In schooling, parent(s) are actively involved in helping young person succeed in school.

7. **Community values youth**—Young person perceives that adults in the community value youth.

8. **Youth as resources**—Young people are given useful roles in the community.

9. **Service to others**—Young person serves in the community one hour or more per week.

10. **Safety**—Young person feels safe at home, at school, and in the neighborhood.

11. **Family boundaries**—Family has clear rules and consequences, and monitors the young person's whereabouts.

12. **School boundaries**—School provides clear rules and consequences.

13. **Neighborhood boundaries**—Neighbors take responsibility for monitoring young people's behavior.

14. **Adult role models**—Parent(s) and other adults model positive, responsible behavior.

15. **Positive peer influence**—Young person's best friends model responsible behavior.

16. **High expectations**—Both parent(s) and teachers encourage the young person to do well.

17. **Creative activities**—Young person spends three or more hours per week in lessons or practice in music, theater, or other arts.

18. **Youth programs**—Young person spends three or more hours per week in sports, clubs, or organizations at school and/or in community organizations.

19. **Religious community**—Young person spends one hour or more per week in activities in a religious institution.

20. **Time at home**—Young person is out with friends "with nothing special to do" two or fewer nights per week.

21. **Achievement motivation**—Young person is motivated to do well in school.

22. **School engagement**—Young person is actively engaged in learning.

23. **Homework**—Young person reports doing at least one hour of homework every school day.

24. **Bonding to school**—Young person cares about her or his school.

25. **Reading for pleasure**—Young person reads for pleasure three or more hours per week.

26. **Caring**—Young person places high value on helping other people.

27. **Equality and social justice**—Young person places high value on promoting equality and reducing hunger and poverty.

28. **Integrity**—Young person acts on convictions and stands up for her or his beliefs.

29. **Honesty**—Young person "tells the truth even when it is not easy."

30. **Responsibility**—Young person accepts and takes personal responsibility.

31. **Restraint**—Young person believes it is important not to be sexually active or to use alcohol or other drugs.

32. **Planning and decision making**—Young person knows how to plan ahead and make choices.

33. **Interpersonal competence**—Young person has empathy, sensitivity, and friendship skills.

34. **Cultural competence**—Young person has knowledge of and comfort with people of different cultural/racial/ethnic backgrounds.

35. **Resistance skills**—Young person can resist negative peer pressure and dangerous situations.

36. **Peaceful conflict resolution**—Young person seeks to resolve conflict nonviolently.

37. **Personal power**—Young person feels he or she has control over "things that happen to me."

38. **Self-esteem**—Young person reports having a high self-esteem.

39. **Sense of purpose**—Young person reports that "my life has a purpose."

40. **Positive view of personal future**—Young person is optimistic about her or his personal future.

Based on data compiled from almost 100,000 sixth to twelfth graders in 213 communities across the United

States, and reported in *Search Institute's Profiles of Student Life: Attitudes and Behaviors,* the average young person surveyed had only 18 of the 40 assets. Other studies, with an even bigger pool to choose from (2,026,891 youth in 2,934 communities), show the same trend. Surprisingly, the number tended to decrease as students got older: Sixth graders reported having 21.5 assets while twelfth graders fell off to only 17.2. While the Institute is careful to note that the list is not to be considered a scientific measure of future success, educators everywhere are starting to pick up on the list as an incredibly useful educational prediction tool. The 40 Developmental Assets™ already have widespread currency among after-school programs. Youth developers across the nation are using the assets to create and improve programming.

To be honest, I had never heard of the 40 Developmental Assets™ until my wife, who has been in the field of education for more than fifteen years, brought them to my attention. Reading the list, I was excited. It was as though chess had been designed to fit many, if not most, of the assets. As is to be expected, not all of the assets directly correlate, but a deeper exploration of parts of the list will demonstrate how chess fits nicely into the overall matrix:

Asset 1: Family support. One of the wonderful things about chess tournaments is the number of parents one sees. Many kids who may not be interested in athletics pick up chess as a way of getting the kind of attention usually received from sports parents. The venue provides an additional opportunity for parents and children to spend some quality time together.

Asset 3: Other adult relationships; Asset 14: Adult role models. As often happens, a relationship with a coach can be extremely important at certain stages of a young person's life. This happens in all sports, and I experienced it with the young people I worked with. In addition, chess has a nice side benefit: It is enjoyed by children and adults alike. You rarely find a sixty-year-old playing basketball with a group of teenagers, but in chess it happens all the time. One of my relationships with an older chess player, Willie Johnson, developed into a lasting friendship. Though twenty years my senior, he is one of my closest friends and godfather to my daughter Nia. It's hard to imagine what natural setting would have brought us together the way our mutual love of chess did.

Adults who play chess can have a positive influence on young people's lives. With the overemphasis on sports figures and entertainers as role models, it seems as if our values have been skewed way off in one direction. The day when chess stars are as popular as basketball players may be far off, but it's well past time that chess and intellectual activities gain general respect in the minds of our youth. When that happens, the nation will be moving in the right direction.

Asset 5: Caring school climate. Principals understand the benefit that intramural sports have on school morale. When any team goes out and competes against other schools, much of the student body tends to rally around their classmates. Of course, if the team wins a national championship, the entire administration will show its pride wholeheartedly. Cheers and pats on the back boost a child's self-esteem and show that the school cares. I've had students get a standing ovation after returning with team and individual trophies from chess tournaments. Naturally, this also goes for teams that don't win it all: In the best school environments, students are shown enthusiastic approval for their effort.

Asset 7: Community values youth; Asset 24: Bonding to school. Often, a chess team's efforts will be showcased to the community at large. In big cities, this is more often done by the mass media. In other cases, the community leaders will invite the champions to special functions. My teams have been congratulated by both Mayor Dinkins and Mayor Giuliani, as well as various assembly members. This kind of reinforcement is invaluable in showing everyone in the community that chess has an important place and that the success of youth is of key importance. The school and community may also show support by working together to raise funds for T-shirts, caps, travel, and room and board. This creates a lasting bond between school and students. A school that cares about the activities of a young person is a school that is cared about.

Asset 15: Positive peer influence. My mom never worried about where I was in the evenings after I got into chess, because she knew I was at a friend's home playing the game we loved. Once kids find a core group of friends who love to do what they do, there is little worry that they will get into trouble copying the negative behavior of young people outside their group. You never hear people saying, "There go those badass chess kids again. I wish they would stay outta my yard!"

Asset 16: High expectations. This asset goes hand in hand with playing chess. Once a child begins to play the game, the adults around him often begin to expect more from him. "Well, if you can play chess, then you must be smart. You should be able to do math, science, or anything else." It's a positive message to send to kids, that nothing but their personal best is expected from them. Standards are established for grades, behavior, attendance, and work habits. Members of my first National Championship team, the Raging Rooks, were able to take these high expectations all the way to the Nationals, to college, and to their current careers. High expectations, supported by love and a show of confidence, almost always lead to the natural fulfillment of a child's potential.

Asset 17: Creative activities. This is the least reported asset among young people (19 percent). Most kids spend little to no time playing chess, practicing music, getting involved with the theater, painting, or other arts. Given that the United States is a society built on individual expression, it's hard to believe that young people spend so little time exploring diverse avenues of individual creativity. The sad conclusion here is that children are engaged in many conformist behaviors that stifle originality, imagination, and inventiveness. An hour of chess a day would be a great antidote to the mindless TV watching and mall hopping that have become the hobbies of choice for many of today's kids.

Asset 18: Youth programs. A mountain of evidence reveals that children who are engaged in youth programs, whether it's being on a sports team, in a club, or a scholastic/community organization, stand a much better chance of avoiding high-risk behavior. It's almost irresponsible to leave high-energy kids to their own devices once the school day is done; the need to do some activity, positive or negative, is too overwhelming. Chess programs operate on the same principle as other popular extracurricular activities. They take place during those dangerous hours between three and six P.M., when most at-risk behaviors occur, and provide a stimulating alternative for young people who are looking for something meaningful to do.

Asset 20: Time at home. A young person who spends three or more nights a week out with friends "with nothing special to do" is likely to find trouble or have trouble find them. I know from my own experience that whenever my friends and I got bored, we started looking for stuff to do, and some of the things we did were not too bright. Once I found chess, I always had something I wanted to do. It kept me playing and studying and off the streets where some of my friends, with no constructive guiding activity, ended up on the wrong side of the law.

Asset 21: Achievement motivation. One of the ongoing criticisms of the National Collegiate Athletic Association (NCAA) is that the focus on the proper development of the student-athlete has been skewed toward the athletic side. More and more, a young person with any measure of physical ability is being pushed to perform on the basketball court, football field, or baseball diamond. This is often to the detriment of their grades. Even players who have little chance of making it in professional sports end up sacrificing their futures chasing the multimillion-dollar contract.

As a big sports fan and a professional chess player myself, I understand the need for practice. It's all a question of balance; the athletics coach must pay more than lip-service to good grades (Coach John Thompson of Georgetown was actually a wonderful example of a coach who sought true balance), the same way a good chess coach will be sure to stress the connections between chess and education. I had a strict rule: Good grades, participation in chess class, and chess ability, in that order. It broke my heart to leave some of my talented players off the team because their grades were not up to snuff. Still, in the long run, I believe this policy benefited not just that child but the whole team. They all got the message that a good education was the most important asset a person could have, no matter what he or she ended up doing in life. After all, even Michael Jordan went back to get his college degree.

Asset 22: School engagement. This is a frequently re-ported asset and it mirrors some of what has already been said. A key point here is the idea that the young person is "actively" engaged in learning. Too often school is a pas-sive affair: The teacher tries to pour in the knowledge that will set into a mold in the child's brain. Unfortunately, this method often leads to lassitude and boredom. Chess learning, on the other hand, strives to be as interactive as possible, compelling the student to think at all times and come up with suggestions, ideas, and solutions as part of the ongoing learning process.

Asset 30: Responsibility/Asset 37: Personal power. One of the great things about playing chess is that the de-cisions are all on the player's shoulders. There is no one else to blame for one's mistakes; only the player moves the pieces. It is sometimes scary for a young person to accept that kind of responsibility; when the inevitable loss comes, there is no easy excuse to make (of course, even chess players run for cover behind lines like "I was sick," or "She's a girl; I let her win"). With a caring coach as guide, the player begins to fully accept himself as the agent of his own loss and develops an internal locus of control. Once he accepts responsibility he can seek ways to address the issues that led to the loss. Only by admit-ting one's own culpability can the player then take the next step toward lasting growth.

This acceptance of responsibility need not be a diffi-cult experience, and it can be an energizing challenge as well. While losses may teach humility, wins produce a sensation of power and control. The principle that bad moves lead to negative consequences and good moves lead to satisfying results is easily transferred to many situations in life, and provides further proof to the young person that he is in control of his own destiny.

As an aside, I'm proud to say that at a time when African-American males are in a state of crisis, most of my chess buddies are dependable family men with children and jobs. I can't point to chess as the only reason for this, but the correlation seems almost self-evident.

Asset 32: Planning and decision making. This one is obviously what chess was made for, and requires no further explanation. Of note, though, is that it ranks near the bottom third on the asset list: It is the twenty-sixth most popular with only 38 percent of kids reporting it. That leaves a whopping 62 percent who feel they have not been trained to be good at making good decisions about their futures. It just shows that these skills are not something that one picks up automatically; they need to be taught in a systematic fashion. Thankfully, young chess players practice this asset on each and every move of each and every game.

Asset 34: Cultural competence. It's impossible to study chess without learning about its international stars. Kids picking up the latest issue of *Chess Life* magazine can't help but read about the Armenian-born world's best, Garry Kasparov, or the Hungarian sensation Judit Polgar. Tournaments are played in exotic locales, some well-known (Paris, London, Beijing, Moscow) and some that most Americans would have difficulty finding on a map (Curaçao, Linares, Wijk aan Zee, Kalmykia). Chess is popular all over the world. At the last Chess Olympiad, there were teams from 125 countries. Go to any major city in Europe and you will find chess being played in schools, clubs, parks, and homes. In tiny Iceland, where Bobby Fischer won his famous match against Boris Spassky, there are more grandmasters per capita than anywhere else in the world. I have had the opportunity to travel the world playing chess, in some cases competing against opponents with whom I couldn't communicate. Our common language of chess was enough; it bridged cultural, racial, and ethnic differences. In a world that is becoming increasingly interconnected, playing chess can help people from diverse backgrounds as they gain respect for one another.

Asset 35: Resistance skills. The number of factors that blend together to allow a young person to resist negative peer pressure and dangerous situations are substantial; many of them have already been listed here (responsibility and personal power, for example). Deserving special mention is the mantra of frustrated parents who, upon seeing their child fall into trouble, often ask, "Why didn't you stop and think?" That simple step could no doubt have saved many youngsters from delinquency, jail, or, in some cases, death. While nothing can guarantee that a child will always make the right decision, any tool that can help a young person to slow down and consider the situation before acting on impulse is worth teaching.

Asset 36: Peaceful conflict resolution. Postgame analysis is a powerful resolution tool. By using a record of the game (notation), the players can discuss the moves, offer insights into what each was thinking during the game, and suggest alternate plans of action for future contests. Though it is rare in any competition to see the two protagonists work together after a game to come to a better understanding of what occurred, it is a common practice in chess. This mutually beneficial process also helps the player who lost deal in a positive way with the feelings of anger and inadequacy by recognizing that the opponent need not be the enemy. In addition, it teaches young people concrete ways to handle emotional situations. Unfortunately, today's sports culture sometimes breeds negative behavior (in hockey, fighting is often an acceptable way to resolve issues). It's not often that you'll see a chess game where a kid reaches back and belts his opponent for delivering checkmate (though, to be honest, I have seen some parents act a little crazy).

Asset 38: Self-esteem. When a young person faces and completes an intricate task, especially one he was not certain to achieve, the resultant feeling of self-confidence is a potent stimulant to future success. Chess offers a young person the opportunity to feel intelligent, creative, capable, self-reliant, disciplined, and a host of other qualities that lead to a strengthening of the child's perception of himself. Even the child who is not a future chess star will feel great about playing one or two good moves. Also, the national rating system (a close-to-accurate gauge of a player's current playing strength) gives every child the opportunity to succeed by allowing him to compete against players at his level. It's no accident that most administrators, teachers, and coaches report a significant boost to self-esteem as one of the biggest benefits to teaching chess to young people.

Asset 39: Sense of purpose. This is an asset that chess shares with a number of other activities. Once a person begins to feel good about how he performs at anything—whether it be school, chess, sports, or even video games—he feels as if life is worth waking up to. Competence breeds desire, desire breeds passion, and passion breeds purpose. The search for a "calling" is one of the most important in any individual's life. It is every parent's responsibility to have a child try many different activities in the hopes that one of them will "inflame the soul." I know from personal experience that chess is a great option, but it's only a start. A sense of purpose is far more transcendent, and is the right of every human being walking the planet.

Asset 40: Positive view of personal future. Of all the assets, this is the one most reported (74 percent), which reflects the eternal optimism of youth. Only distinctly negative, bordering on traumatic, life experiences will cause children to see mainly darkness ahead. Still, as powerful as the childhood sense of hope is, it thirsts for reinforcement from as many sources as possible. Intriguingly, youngsters who begin to play chess often raise their expectations for their future. One of my former students tells it best: "My life had been going pretty badly for a long time. I used to get physically abused a lot. I stopped caring about the pain, about anything. Then I had a life-altering experience and decided to change my life for the better. Chess was one of the things that I loved doing. It made me feel great and gave me a sense that I could do anything I wanted to do."

I can see why my wife was so excited to have me see this list. By itself, chess strongly correlates with at least twenty-two of the assets. Note once again that the average child reported having only eighteen. The developmental assets list provides one of the most independent and objective measures of the desirability of chess in the nation's scholastic system.

Bloom's Taxonomy

On my educational landscape, questions are more important than answers: knowledge and, more important, understanding should evolve from the constant probing of such questions.

—HOWARD GARDNER, *THE DISCIPLINED MIND*

One of the most compelling scientific explanations for the benefits of teaching chess in the classroom lies in the widely accepted educational framework known as Bloom's Taxonomy. In 1956, Benjamin Bloom headed a group of psychologists who developed a classification of levels of intellectual behavior important in learning. This taxonomy contained three overlapping domains: cognitive, affective, and psychomotor. Within the cognitive domain, Bloom's team was able to identify six levels: knowledge, comprehension, application, analysis, synthesis, and evaluation. Within these levels are the various activities associated with each:

1. ***Knowledge:*** Acquaintance with facts, truth, and principles. To demonstrate knowledge, one has to memorize, recall, define, duplicate, list, recognize, and repeat.
2. ***Comprehension:*** Understanding; the power to grasp ideas. To demonstrate comprehension, one has to explain, describe, express, restate, select, and translate.
3. ***Application:*** The act of putting to a special use or purpose. Application requires one to demonstrate, use, illustrate, interpret, operate, practice, and solve.
4. ***Analysis:*** The process of studying the nature of something or of determining its essential features and their relations. This method of thinking requires one to appraise, calculate, compare, contrast, criticize, differentiate, disassemble, examine, experiment, question, and test.
5. ***Synthesis:*** The combining of constituent elements into a single or unified entity. To carry out this procedure, one must assemble, formulate, prepare, plan, compose, construct, design, develop, formulate, organize, and create.
6. ***Evaluation:*** The act of determining the quality of something. This procedure requires one to appraise, assess, argue, compare, estimate, judge, predict, rate, and value.

The following diagram illustrates the various tiers of Bloom's Taxonomy in order of importance, starting from the bottom up.

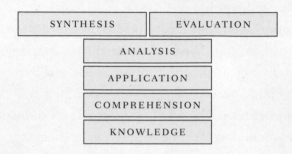

Bloom found that over 95 percent of the test questions students encounter require them to think only at the lowest possible level . . . the recall of information. This is reflected in teachers asking such questions as: Who? What? Where? When? and How many? While this testing of knowledge is important, its rampant overuse limits the development of critical thinking skills in students. Instead, Bloom suggested questions such as: How can . . . ? How would . . . ? How could . . . ? What if . . . ? as ways to encourage students to use their higher mental faculties.

While over forty years of research has confirmed the validity of Bloom's Taxonomy, the broader educational establishment has found it challenging to implement its principles. This is due in large part to the fact that it's simply easier to test for knowledge, where responses easily fit into true or false categories. However, a sea of research has shown that children remember far more when they learn to manage the topic at the higher cognitive levels. This is due to the brain's natural capacity to make connections in multiple locations, according to the connectionist theory model first proposed by David Rumelhart and James McClelland in 1986 and revisited in *Scientific American* in 2000. Other theories have pointed out that requiring students to deeply elaborate on information they are given further embeds the knowledge in long-term memory.

While some thought may need to be given as to exactly how one uses Bloom's Taxonomy to teach subjects such as Spanish or the Civil War, it seems as if chess was invented with Bloom in mind. It is almost impossible for a child to play a game of chess (well or poorly) without carrying out every mental operation listed on the chart. Let's take a closer look at some of the ways Bloom's Taxonomy works in chess.

♟ KNOWLEDGE

On the most basic level, a child must demonstrate a thorough knowledge of all the rules of the game, including the slightly esoteric *en passant* and *underpromotion* (see Glossary). Later, the students will learn the opening moves, memorize famous games, master basic endgames, and recognize typical checkmates.

This raw acquisition of knowledge does not cease even for grandmasters, as professionals need to keep up-to-date on the latest innovations being played by their colleagues around the world. I recall winning a game against British master Jonathan Ady in which we played the exact opening moves to a game played just the day before by two of the world's best players. I had happened to see the moves over the Internet that morning and for the first several moves I merely mimicked the ideas of the winning side. By the time my opponent realized what was going on, he was already in deep trouble. After I had won the game, I asked him if he had seen the game from the day before and he quickly shook his head no. Thanks to that bit of knowledge I would later go on to take the final step to becoming grandmaster.

♟ COMPREHENSION

Despite the above anecdote, it is not enough for chess players simply to know moves; it is more important to know why those moves need to be played. Take the opening moves, for example. The most famous first move, the one World Champion Bobby Fischer used to call best by test, is for the player with the white pieces to push the pawn in front of his king's two squares. It is entirely possible to play this move, and ten subsequent ones, from memory, without having a clue as to what makes them powerful. Essentially, this is what a computer does, as it has no ability (yet) to understand the reasons behind its actions. However, sooner or later, given the enormous complexity of chess, a new move will be played that will make all prior knowledge irrelevant. If the player has not fully grasped the purpose behind all his previous moves, mistakes will naturally follow.

A good friend of mine once asked me a question about a game he lost in which he thought he had made a big mistake very early on. He showed me the first twelve moves, remarking that it was all to be found in books. His problem arose when his opponent played a move that was not in the book. What was his response? To play as if nothing new had happened. Naturally, the landscape had dramatically shifted and the move he played had nothing at all to do with what was happening on the board. He was soon ground to a pulp. (I can say that. He's a really good friend!)

This is one of the dangers of knowledge: We rely on it even when the situation demands that we remain flexible and adopt a totally new strategy. Only by understanding the reasons behind every action can we begin to avoid the fiasco that my friend stepped into. I would always tout the importance of truly understanding every move to my students. On many occasions, this saved them from some truly scary positions in important tournaments. I recall one game at the 1991 Nationals in Dearborn, Michigan, where one of the eighth graders I was coaching had such a horrible position after the first few moves I couldn't bear to watch. I left the playing hall, walked around a bit, and later decided to return to see how he was doing.

The shift was dramatic; not only had he turned the game around, he was now dominating his opponent from every angle. After he had won the game, I asked him how he had felt after having such a terrible position initially. "I was scared," he replied. "The guy was playing so fast, like he knew everything. But then, when I made a move he didn't know, he started playing bad. I'm amazed how easy it was to win after that."

♟ APPLICATION

One of the beauties of chess is that students are forced to demonstrate their knowledge and understanding on every single move. All the study in the world means nothing; it's what happens over the board that truly counts. In tournaments, there is the additional challenge of doing it under pressure from a dangerous opponent, and with a clock curtailing thinking time. The rush that chess players get from the challenge of having to prove what they know keeps drawing more and more adherents to the game. Kids also develop an enhanced sense of self as they successfully show their skills time and time again.

One of my great pleasures as an instructor is to see the joy on a kid's face after he has won a game using an idea I taught. It is a look of satisfaction, amazement, and slight disbelief that ideas can be filled with such power and meaning. This almost always leads to a hunger to know more, for me to teach something new. The interplay between chess knowledge/understanding and immediate application paradoxically makes chess one of the easiest subjects to teach to young people.

I can recall a great example of this when I taught my students a new opening, the Sveshnikov Variation of the Sicilian Defense. It is a complex opening series of moves, where the player with the black pieces allows his pawn alignment to be compromised while his other forces gain an incredible amount of activity. Despite the unusual setup, Brian Watson, one of my better players, took to it like a duck to water. He started winning game after game with the opening, so much so that his confidence level went through the roof. None of his teammates could touch him. Even Charu Robinson, a top player from the year before, who had since graduated, was dumbfounded at how skilled Brian had become. "He was just dumb nice," said Charu. "I was amazed at how good he had gotten. And his understanding of the Svesnikov was incredible."

In the 1992 New York State Scholastic Championships, Brian used the opening to effect, dominating the competition and winning first place outright. After his victory we were giddy with excitement; to see new knowledge applied so forcefully and effectively is one of the greatest feelings a child, or a coach, can have. And it's one that occurs in chess almost daily.

♟ ANALYSIS

Chess really begins to work its magic the moment a child learns how to analyze. Initially, a young player will often lash out, playing the first attractive move that comes to mind. In some cases, this happens even after many months of play. However, sooner or later, as poor moves are consistently and ruthlessly punished, the student begins to slow down (miracle!), to show patience (no way!), and to carefully calculate the different options before making a move (a parent's dream!). This search for alternatives is a great counterpoint to a scholastic system that most often encourages kids to look for just one right answer. In chess there often isn't just one right move. In one and the same position, Bobby Fischer might make one move while Garry Kasparov might play something else. Former world championship contender David Bronstein told a story about sitting around with ten other grandmasters watching a hotly contested game between two of their colleagues. For fun, the group decided to see if they could guess the moves the players would make. Bronstein was stunned to see how many disagreements occurred. It made him realize that the search for the one right answer did not always work or maybe even matter. The point is that there could be multiple ways to approach an issue, and although these great chess minds often disagreed as to which method was best, that did not prevent them from winning their individual games.

As I mentioned before, analysis demands patience. One of the more dramatic examples I've ever seen of a kid learning how to slow down and check out the various options was at a national championship in Tucson, Arizona. It was round one of the tournament, and I had just given all the students my big speech about how we coaches would be incredibly proud of them if they just gave their best for the team. I sent them off on an emotional high, and settled back in a chair for what I suspected would be at least an hour or so before they began to finish their games. Within fifteen minutes, in sauntered ten-year-old Chris Peralta, smiling from ear to ear.

"What happened?" I asked.

"I won," he replied, beaming.

"That was a quick game. Was it easy?"

"No. It took eighty moves."

I was stunned. He handed me the two score sheets that he had used to record the moves of the game. The first was filled, front to back, and the other was almost half full. I made a quick calculation: He had made eighty moves, and so had his opponent. It had taken them fifteen minutes (900 seconds) to play 160 moves between them. On top of that, he had managed to record the entire game, which cut into his thinking time. That meant they had probably used two or three seconds on each move. This was certainly not the best way to win a national championship.

"Why did you move so quickly?" I asked.

"I won," he replied, not expecting my question.

"Yes, Chris. I'm happy that you won. But you hardly stopped to think."

"Okay. But neither did my opponent."

"That doesn't matter. Your teammates are counting on you. Look around. You're the only one out here. They're still in there playing, taking their time. As fast as you moved, you could just as easily have lost the game."

"But I won!" he protested.

"Good. But you won't keep winning if you keep playing that quickly."

Then, unexpectedly, Chris burst into tears. I was shocked. Here I was trying to properly coach him, and instead I felt like a big bully. Of course, all he wanted was my approval, and being criticized for his first win at his first Nationals was not a gratifying feeling. I had to backpedal and remind him that I was proud of his win, but that I was worried about how he was going to feel if he kept playing that quickly and lost his next few games. He wiped his tears and nodded his head in acknowledgment. I wasn't quite sure if he had gotten it, but I was relieved that he was feeling better.

The next round, I stressed to the group that even if they didn't win, I would be extremely proud of each and every one of them if they took their time and analyzed the different possibilities of each move. I told them that that would mean as much to me as winning a national championship.

Chris left for the game with a twinkle in his eye. An hour passed and there was no sign of Chris. Two hours went by, and most of the other kids had finished their games. It was well into the third hour, and with all the other games finished, Chris finally came into the room. I didn't need to know how his game had ended; the look we gave each other said it all. To be honest, I don't even remember what the result was, though I'm fairly certain he won. The scene was repeated again and again until the end of the championship as Chris was almost always one of the last kids to leave the playing hall. While he did not win all of his games, when the smoke had cleared, my little rookie had the best score of anyone on our team in that division. By taking his time, delving into moves and countermoves in the search for effective ideas, he had changed from a kid who can play good moves to one whose plans had greater depth and accuracy. The improvement in his game was dramatic, so much so that, by the following year, Chris had become captain of the team. The power of analysis took a child with raw skills and honed him into a fierce competitor, without adding any more knowledge to the equation.

♟ SYNTHESIS

Once a thorough analysis has been done, it is time to synthesize the information. This may involve creating a new idea from all the information one has gathered. Or it may require the drafting of a plan of action that perfectly fits the situation. It is a quality that demands independent thinking and confidence in one's own abilities, and is the hallmark of really creative thinking.

A high-level example of this was seen in the 1990 World Chess Championships between the champion Garry Kasparov and his archrival Anatoly Karpov. In game fourteen of the match, Kasparov wheeled out the little-used Scotch Opening, long considered to be a tame way to play. Kasparov, however, had studied it carefully, and had a few new ideas in store. Although he only managed to draw the first time he used it, he won the next game and subsequently the entire match. He then used the opening on other rivals, introducing twists and turns no one had thought of before. This led to a complete renaissance of the opening, as everyone wanted to jump on the bandwagon of the new and interesting ideas Kasparov had infused into the play. It was Kasparov's undying creativity, and his consummate ability to synthesize old material by adding a new flavor, that kept him at the undisputed top of world chess for over fifteen years.

One exercise I would do with my students was to hand them a combination of chess pieces, say a rook and two pawns, and challenge them to create their own checkmates. This not only required them to reference what they already knew about checkmates, but that they use that knowledge to create something fresh and original. It didn't matter if the idea was new in the grand scheme of things; it only mattered that it was new to them. The exercise promoted independent thinking, and the process of discovery and invention bred a measure of confidence that pushed them to greater heights.

♟ EVALUATION

One of the greatest skills to teach anyone is the ability to distinguish between quality and garbage. Saturated as we are with media, videos, and political spins, our ability to evaluate takes on mind-saving importance. In chess, the act is just as rigorously needed, as all moves and countermoves have to be held to the highest standard. Ideas and situations have to be assessed fairly accurately, as the slightest misjudgment might lead to an overestimation of one's chances.

It may be this ability to keenly evaluate a position that most separates a weak chess player from a strong one. Professionals can often glance at a setup and decide which side, black or white, stands better, and why. In the experiment by Adriaan de Groot cited earlier, the scientist found that grandmasters did not often look more moves ahead than lower-ranking experts; it was their fine-tuned chess sense that made them sniff out the qualitatively better moves and focus on those alone. Without the ability to make consistent, high-level evaluations, weaker players actually end up spending more time looking at more irrelevant possibilities.

This need to evaluate well is so critical to chess success that grandmasters have developed certain survival methods to help keep them objective. A recent study published by the journal *Nature* reported the findings of two cognitive scientists, Michelle Cowley and Ruth Byrne of Trinity College Dublin, who were studying how different chess players described how their current moves would affect their position in the long run. They found that novices often argued in favor of their bad moves by suggesting only poor countermoves for their opponents. Masters, however, were more pessimistic (some might say realistic), because they looked for only the strongest responses from opponents.

"Grand masters think about what their opponents will do much more," said Byrne. "They tend to falsify their own hypotheses." Basically, a grand master will often ask the question, "In what ways might this idea be wrong?"

According to Cowley and Byrne, this act of falsification of one's own ideas is found as a primary method of evaluation only among strong chess players and scientists.

While other fields—law being a great example—try to disprove their colleagues's ideas all the time, it is only within these two fields that huge chunks of time are spent trying to poke holes in one's own best ideas. The authors of the study assert that more research is needed to determine how and when this happens for chess players as they improve through the ranks, but, for our purposes, this example shows that the act of playing chess regularly contributes to the kind of higher-order thinking that is generally very difficult to develop. The constant obligation to assess, critique, predict, and justify every move in a game places the demand for quality control on the player's ideas. Students of the game quickly learn, as former world champion Emanuel Lasker once said, that "on the chessboard, lies and hypocrisy do not survive long."

Knowledge, comprehension, application, analysis, synthesis, and evaluation often interweave simultaneously during a chess game. There is often no dividing line, which is as it should be. Thinking is an ever-changing dynamic act, like the shifting patterns of fast-moving clouds. The important thing is that chess challenges students to stretch their minds in ways that will be useful in school and in life. Those who doubt that this transference is happening simply have not looked at the evidence, both anecdotal and scientific.

Bloom's Taxonomy is finally leaving its theoretical roots and is gaining an ever-greater presence in the nation's largest public school systems. My sister-in-law, who is currently pursuing her teacher's certification, has had to integrate it into her work. It's my hope that as this tool becomes more established, educators will see that chess is an ideal way to help develop these higher-order cognitive functions. Given the data showing how chess has helped thousands of kids around the globe to improve their critical thinking skills, it would be madness for its inclusion in the general curriculum to be far behind.

♟ CONCLUSION

This quartet of measurements—studies, flow, developmental assets, and Bloom's Taxonomy—forms a convincing case as to the virtues of including chess in the educational system. The data provide a strong refutation to those who claim that chess is just a game, merely a diversion from real learning. Naturally, chess is by no means a miraculous panacea for all the ills that plague our schools. But as a discipline, chess has been proven many times over to make dramatic improvements in the lives of young people.

Four

CHESS

AND

SCHOOLS

My Experience
as an Educator

I slept and dreamt that life was Joy, and then I awoke and
realized that life was Duty; And then I went to work—
and, lo and behold, I discovered that Duty can be Joy.
—RABINDRANATH TAGORE

The first day I walked into a classroom as a chess-instruc-
tor-in-training at Roberto Clemente Elementary School in
the Bronx, I knew I had come home.

I had been offered a job by the American Chess Foundation (ACF) to teach inner-city kids the basics of the
game. Being in college at the time, I jumped at the chance
to earn a few extra bucks on the side, especially since
chess masters at my level were being paid an astounding
fifty dollars an hour. Even though I would only be working
a few hours a week and in some of the roughest neighborhoods in the city, I decided that I probably could not find
a better situation. Little did I know I had found my mission in life, or, more accurately, my mission had found me.

Doug Bellizi, a chess master and coach for the ACF,

had brought me along to watch a class, and had just begun to conduct a lesson in front of thirty bright young
Black and Latino faces. I had not been inside an elementary school since my days in Jamaica; the kids showed an
effervescence that was absolutely contagious. I smiled at
them and they smiled back. Their desire to learn lit up the
room.

I sat on the side and watched as Doug stood in front
of a large hanging replica of a chess set (known as a
demonstration board) and tried to explain the goals of
opening play. It was a basic lesson, the logic of which is
that if the kids learn to handle the first few moves compe-
tently, they would be ready to play a decent game. Doug
had barely gone two minutes into the importance of development (getting the pieces off the back row and into the
struggle), when the noise level in the room began to rise.
As he talked, most of the kids ignored him. I was shocked
as these little angels, with their regular teacher happily on
a break somewhere in the building, talked, laughed at
jokes, and called each other names. I glanced up at Doug,
who every so often gave a mild shush, but by and large focused on trying to finish his next point, this one about the
importance of castling. Maybe 20 percent of the class
paid attention, and *they* probably retained 5 percent of
what he was saying. My initial excitement quickly turned
to disappointment: at the children for misbehaving, and at
Doug for letting them get away with it.

After about ten minutes, when the rumbling threatened to turn into random chaos, Doug finally chimed,
"Okay, let's take out the chessboards." Suddenly, the kids

squealed with delight. Shouts of "Yes!" peppered the room, and Doug smiled as he placed the plastic chess sets and vinyl boards at each table. Eager hands snapped at the pieces, and full belly laughs followed bad moves. One child would move a rook like a bishop, and another would play by checker rules, wiping out two or three pieces in one move, while Doug wandered from table to table correcting mistakes and offering warm encouragement. The pure joy of play had descended on the room, and I found myself laughing at this comedic reminder of why I fell in love with chess in the first place. By the time the bell had rung, the class seemed to have reveled in the experience and was clamoring for more. Still, something about it bothered me, and it was only reinforced as Doug and I left the school and talked.

"These kids face tremendous challenges," he said. "Poverty, drugs in the neighborhood, broken homes. You can understand why sometimes their attention span isn't great. If we're going to give them all the benefits that chess has to offer, I find that you have to be real patient with them."

I looked at Doug. Here was this white guy trudging all the way up to the South Bronx to teach inner city kids a fourteen-hundred-year-old game. It was obviously a labor of love, a firm belief that what he was doing was so powerful that it would help to make a difference in the life of any child. He would later go on to oversee the Right Move program, a series of free tournments designed to give the rigors of serious play to kids who have trouble affording the entry fees. But while his intentions were pure, I could not accept his approach. I had been one of those kids and I knew that I had wanted one thing more than anything else; to be meaningfully challenged. To be honest, I never got to see Doug's follow-up classes to see if he ramped up the difficulty level. My instincts, and my youthful impatience, just told me that the slow piecemeal method was not for me.

I quickly realized that since the kids were enthusiastic, teaching them general opening strategy was not the best method. The first thing to do was to engage them. All kids want to feel smart; that surge of confidence from knowing the right answers to questions and getting adult approval for it is a universal drug for kids from all cultures.

I decided to plan my lessons differently. When I was finally assigned my first group—a bunch of eager sixth graders at P.S. 123 in Harlem—I decided to skip the opening of the game entirely and teach them the rudiments of the endgame. This involved showing them popular checkmates: how to win with a queen, a single rook, or both rooks and how to turn a lowly pawn into the most feared piece on the board. I asked them plenty of questions at each step, a method that had them fully engaged the moment I entered the classroom. The concrete skills I taught gave them the ability to finish off their opponents consistently, which naturally infused them with a feeling of immediate power. In every game they played, the checkmates I taught them magically appeared; they loved nothing more than to show me how they had dusted off an opponent using a technique they had just learned.

Seeing how successful my method was proving to be,

I continued to work backward, showcasing the middle-game, with all its exciting tactics that allowed one side to set deadly traps for the opponent to fall into. Often, the result would be the win of an important piece, and the kids quickly came to understand that losing a piece for nothing in return was just about the worst thing one could do in a chess game. Everything I showed them had immediate application, and, as their games confirmed the veracity of my teachings, they began to eagerly anticipate my next lesson. By the time I had gotten around to explaining the general strategy of openings (Doug's original lesson), they were hanging on every word.

The ACF sent me to a number of schools around Harlem, and the results were the same. Teachers would come to me in wide-eyed amazement, wondering how I was getting their classes so wired up about learning. I would get special pleasure out of getting "problem" kids who were incredibly disruptive in their regular classes to sit still and focus when it came time for chess. I enjoyed the attention from the teachers, but I knew that it wasn't me: Few young kids could resist touching the chess pieces, which naturally made them inquire about what the pieces could do. Once that happened, they were as good as hooked.

Still, the teachers' bewilderment made me reflect on the disconnect some kids were having in school and the attachment they quickly had for chess. I sensed that there was something about the school system itself that was turning these kids off, as teachers struggled with old books, inadequate funding, and serious family problems spilling over into the classroom. But I also sensed that there was something more, something fundamentally missing in the teachers' approach that made them fail to reach a number of kids.

It soon became fairly evident to me that the kids enjoyed learning chess because, in this case, knowledge was indeed power. What you didn't know could get you checkmated. This was applicable knowledge: You learn a new move or idea and ten minutes later you use it to beat your friend, or to fend off his attack. Most subjects in school didn't even pretend to have that profound connection between what children were learning and in what ways that information could be readily used. The abstract idea of knowledge for knowledge's sake, as important as that was and is, turned off many kids. I remember always gravitating to the teachers who showed me why what I was learning was important instead of just telling me about it. Fascinating subjects like American history lost all their intrigue when reduced to facts and dates, completely unrelated to our real lives. The magical word here was connection: Connect anything to something meaningful to kids and they will listen with rapt attention. It was something I understood intuitively, and it was something that chess almost naturally offered.

I say "almost" naturally because even some chess coaches did not see chess's power to the full extent that I did. They saw the effectiveness of showing a kid a new checkmate or a nice opening variation. But many believed that it stopped there, that chess was just about chess. Even those who saw the many life links did not necessarily try to make it part of their lessons. To me, the opposite was true: Chess was everywhere. Its many strategic insights proved useful when applied to life, and the discipline it demanded strengthened the minds of the young people who studied and played it. I saw how mastering chess had affected my own life, and I wanted to spread the word to every kid I taught.

In addition, in those neighborhoods where toughness often meant survival, chess seemed to fit right in. There was an element of hand-to-hand combat, where one move could be the difference between life and death. All the kids—tough, average, nerdy—could relate to the game; it spoke to their experiences. They didn't need for me to preach it to them; they knew people (their own family members in some cases) who were suffering the consequences of wrong moves, poor choices, and bad decisions. Chess had immediacy to it. "You mess up, you lose, son!" There was no forgiveness and no reliance on luck. Winning demanded a tiger's mentality, and each time a kid, no matter how meek in life, won a game, he felt as though he had proven himself in some fundamental way he could not fully explain.

But the kids also saw that there was much more to chess than it just being a conduit for aggression and an opportunity to defeat an opponent. There were important lessons to be learned as well. There were times when a poor move was not so terrible as to cost the whole game. In those cases, the player who kept his cool and bolstered all the tenacity he could muster often turned the tables against an overconfident opponent. It was a powerful lesson for the kids to see that bad moves did not always lose. But even in losses, they began to see the potential for their own personal growth. There proved to be a redemptive quality to failure. A fatal blunder in chess only cost one game. The error could be analyzed, poked, prodded, discussed, and even laughed at. They soon saw that mistakes were not the sin—not learning from them was. After a loss, one could wipe the slate clean, set up the pieces and play again, this time with greater wisdom. What doesn't kill you will make you strong. My job was to be a facilitator to these realizations; a few words of consolation from me could turn a bad loss into a life lesson learned. The kids were savvy enough to fill in the blanks.

I constantly tried to instill in the kids a love and respect for the game. I would review famous battles from as early as the 1860s when such superstars as Paul Morphy and Adolf Anderssen used to dominate world chess. They began to see and appreciate the poetry of a well-played game, the subtle musical artistry that rivaled a Beethoven sonata, or the back-and-forth flow that resembled a hot hip-hop beat. I would punctuate games with excited commentary: "Juice!" was one of my favorite exclamations, reserved for a move that shattered an opponent's position and sent his army reeling. The kids started to look for "juice moves" because they knew that would get me excited and the room abuzz. Discovering an excellent move was like making a no-look pass in basketball, and each kid eagerly wanted to show off his skills. Some moves produced the kind of twisted faces reserved for Michael Jordan dunks, stuff so nasty that we thought it wasn't even right that someone had gotten abused like that. Students would be so engrossed in the lessons that the bell would ring without them getting a chance to play. So much for short attention spans.

The excitement did not stop in the classroom. Once the kids discovered chess tournaments, with gleaming trophies going to the victors, their motivation went through the roof. We started to hold in-school tournaments to give as many students as possible the opportunity to participate. In most cases, we tried to make sure each child went home with something—a trophy, medallion, T-shirt, or certificate of participation—to show off to a proud parent. The success of these events naturally led some schools to want to send their stars to test their blossoming skills against kids around the city. While we always sought to get money to take big groups, the reality of inadequate financial resources forced us to limit the number of students we took to the more elite tournaments. The competition to be chosen to represent a school would be fierce: students had to keep their grades up, receive no disciplinary measures from their teachers, and be good chess players. A good percentage of my better chess players were drawn to chess because it stimulated them in ways school did not. Those were the kids I was most passionate about reaching; as long as they showed effort and improvement in their classes, I could not turn them away. I always had a special place in my heart for the children who no one paid much attention to, but who would rock all challengers on the chessboard. Maybe they reminded me of myself.

Though I enjoyed teaching in most schools, two programs in particular really stood out. The first was at Adam Clayton Powell Jr. Junior High School (also known as J.H.S. 43) on 129th Street and Amsterdam Avenue in Central Harlem. I ended up at the school because a few of my elementary school stars from P.S. 123 had graduated and were now attending. We were fortunate that there was a dedicated science teacher, Richard Gudonsky, on staff, and he happened to love chess. Before I had arrived, he would keep his door open twice a week during lunch and invite the teens to come into his room to play. He had a sporadic following of about four or five kids, but when my group showed up in the fall of 1989, his ad hoc chess club tripled in size. On meeting me Mr. Gudonsky was humble and unassuming.

"You are a chess master," he said. "What can I do to help you help the kids?"

When I told him the students needed to practice on the days when I wasn't around, he immediately complied by opening his room five days a week at lunchtime. When it came time for the team to go to competitions on the weekends, he would drive from Queens to Harlem at five in the morning to pick up each child, drive them to tournaments all over Manhattan, wait all day until they finished, and then drive them back home in the evening. His selfless sacrifice was as much a major part of those students' success as anything I ever did for them over the chessboard.

With such a loving combination, the team at J.H.S. 43 turned into a powerhouse, winning tournament after tournament in the New York City area before going on to tie for first in the 1991 National Junior High School Championships. Their story appeared on the front page of the *New York Times* with the headline "Harlem Teenagers Checkmate a Stereotype." For a time, the Raging Rooks (as they called themselves) were treated like stars, even getting a call down to City Hall to be feted by then mayor David Dinkins. Two of the top Rooks eventually got scholarships to prestigious Manhattan private schools: Charu Robinson attended the prestigious Dalton School and Dwayne Brian Watson went the following year to the Day School. In both cases, their grades were not of paramount importance: It was the potential they showed as chess champions that got them the scholarships.

The massive media attention the team received showed just how potent stereotypes can be. Juxtaposing chess with inner-city youth came as a shock to many in the press who themselves were intimidated by the game. One of the most common questions I was asked, often with a look of befudded wonder, was "How do you motivate these kids to play chess?" I could hear the echo of the underlying assumptions: that chess was akin to rocket science and that minority kids would prefer to play basketball. Charu may have said it best when he commented that we were being treated like a Cinderella team. Naturally, rags-to-riches stories make for great press. My take was that as long as the kids benefited without anything negative being said about them, then we should take as much media coverage as we could get.

I would replicate the success of the Raging Rooks at

Mott Hall, a middle school, located just three blocks away at 131st Street and Convent Avenue. The program was sponsored by philanthropist Dan Rose through his non-profit organization, the Harlem Educational Activities Fund (HEAF), whose focus was on a variety of scholarly and enrichment activities that helped stimulate the young people of Central Harlem and Washington Heights. I became involved at the school when the principal, Mirian Acosta-Sing, cornered me in a restaurant and insisted that I come to her building. Her enthusiasm and the support of HEAF made it very easy for me to latch onto their mission of excellence for young people.

What started as a small group of about thirteen kids after school eventually expanded to the entire incoming class. The demand was so great that I had to bring in help: Jerald Times, a chess master I had known for years, and, a few years later, two of my graduates from the Raging Rooks championship team, Kasaun Henry (team captain) and Charu. The team, which called themselves the Dark Knights, became a powerhouse on the Junior Varsity circuit, winning back-to-back championships in 1994 and 1995. Three of my students also became individual national champions in those years, while many others invariably finished in the top ten in their division. The Knights also got an audience with a New York City mayor, this time Rudolph Giuliani. Three world champions would visit the school to play against the students—Garry Kasparov, Anatoly Karpov, and the women's world champion Susan Polgar, who HEAF recruited to spend a year teaching at the school. Many of the students have since gone on to Yale, Harvard, New York University, and other top universities. When I see them now, they all speak about the amazing effect learning chess at a young age had on their lives.

I took a break from coaching in 1997 to pursue my life-long goal of becoming an international grandmaster. With the generous financial assistance of Mr. Rose, who was grateful I had led so many of his teams to prominent national titles, I was able to take on a more supervisory role with the team while I put in rigorous hours of daily study. Since achieving the title in 1999, I have been able to spread the word about chess on a national level, traveling to cities all over the United States to speak to groups of young people about the benefits of chess. The message is slowly spreading. My dream is to see chess in every school in America. It will take time, but there are signs that it's starting to happen.

A Profile of
Three Programs

*Avoid the crowd. Do your own thinking independently. Be
the chess player, not the chess piece.*

—RALPH CHARELL, AUTHOR

With the compelling and comprehensive proof of the
scholastic benefits of chess now coming to light, it is no
wonder that teachers and administrators across the
United States have begun to incorporate chess into the
nation's classrooms. In almost every major city, there is at
least one in-school or after-school chess program focused
on using the game to develop character and discipline in
young people as well as act as an effective tool of interven-
tion. Movies like *Searching for Bobby Fischer* and *Harry
Potter: The Chamber of Secrets* (with its use of a magical
chess set) have made chess even more appealing, further
helping to erase the idea that it's a nerdy activity in the
minds of today's kids. And more and more, politicians are
backing bills to make chess a part of the school curriculum. Here are just three of the model programs that are

leading the effort of bringing chess to America's young people.

♟ CHESS-IN-THE-SCHOOLS (NEW YORK, NEW YORK)

Located on the second floor an office building on the corner of Eighth Avenue and Thirty-seventh Street, the Chess-in-the-Schools (CIS) organization is an homage to chess. Upon exiting the elevator, visitors are treated to huge black-and-white photos of young people in deep concentration over chessboards. The theme of chess is everywhere, especially in the red-and-white-checkered squares that dominate the walls and high ceilings. The wall in the main conference room features, in algebraic notation, a famous game won by the future champion Bobby Fischer against Grandmaster Donald Byrne when the prodigy was only fourteen. A special room is dedicated to packing and storing chess sets, ready and waiting to be delivered to schools clamoring to fill the needs of kids hungry to be a part of the chess program.

"We can't do it all," says Marley Kaplan, president and CEO of CIS, when I talked to her over the phone. "We have over a hundred schools on our waiting list and we already serve 38,000 kids. Principals are calling us all the time. I guess that means the word is out that we've got a good thing going."

Since its inception in 1986, CIS (formerly the American Chess Foundation) has reached over 300,000 kids.

With the success of the Raging Rooks and other teams, the demand for chess in the city and nationwide exploded.

"We tried to be all things to all people," says Lewis Cullman, chairman of the board. "We didn't want to turn anyone down. But the excitement for chess has been growing exponentially, and overseeing that entire effort is difficult for one organization to do. We realized pretty quickly that we can be the leaders, the prototype for everyone to follow. I think by doing such a great job in New York City, we've been able to motivate the whole country to see what a great teaching tool chess really is."

In 1997, the organization began a systematic plan tailored to serving city schools that are Title I, meaning that 35 percent or more students in each school qualify for free or subsidized breakfast and lunches. The growth was massive in terms of the number of kids they were able to connect with: 12,000 in 1997, 18,000 in 1998, 22,000 in 1999, and 30,000 in 2000. Now at a comfortable 38,000 over the past four years, the focus is on adding more depth to each individual program through more lessons and tournaments. With 160 schools, the challenge is huge. "We certainly could use more funding," pitches Kaplan.

Still, they've had a remarkable level of success. CIS is known nationwide in all chess education circles. Teams from their programs have won several national championship titles despite facing well-trained opposition from public and private schools all over the country. Coaches, books, and chess materials are sent to each CIS school at no cost to the school. Instruction takes place year-round in a variety of programs. A sixteen-week intensive course is offered as part of the regular school day, with a follow-up after-school component for the more motivated players.

A summer program takes advantage of the full availability of the kids' being off from school. For many CIS students, the humid months of July and August are lost to TV watching or trying to stay cool at open johnny pumps. With so few meaningful alternatives, chess has been an ideal way to pass the time productively.

A recent addition to the summer activities is daily lessons at Camp Ramapo in Rhinebeck, New York, where more than nine hundred disadvantaged New York City children with special needs can learn chess from five CIS alumni high school students. The children are referred by agencies and have various personal challenges, some as severe as autism. The days are incredibly regimented and include all sorts of fun outdoor activities. There is one period, one day a week, when the kids are given the option to choose whatever activity they wish. On average, 75 percent pick chess.

Kaplan takes a special thrill in relating stories like this. "It's not a surprise, but it's always amazing," she says. "Here are kids who could be doing anything else, and they choose chess."

With so many kids coming through the program, there are hundreds of inspiring stories. Kaplan recalls one youngster whose story warms her heart every time she recalls it:

"His name is Chris Escobar. His father passed away when he was young, and then, just when he started learning chess, his mom passed away. He will tell you, chess saved him." When I asked if I could get in touch with him, Kaplan, without mentioning the significance of CIS's continued dedication to their kids, transferred me to Chris, who is now interning at CIS while studying at the Borough of Manhattan Community College in downtown Manhattan. His voice came across as confident and composed, and his own words about his life with chess, his mom passing, and his hopes for the future are a living testament to the role chess played in his life:

I grew up in a really tough neighborhood on the Lower East Side. A lot of my friends dropped out of high school. They're having kids right now and they're only eighteen years old. They're in the streets selling drugs, not doing anything with their lives. If not for chess, I might be in the same predicament.

The coaches at CIS, they always stayed on your back to stay in school, making sure you got good grades, checking in constantly on how you're doing. With chess, it helps toward discipline in school, just to sit down and concentrate, to be able to take things apart little by little.

When I was a little kid I was so hyper, especially in elementary school. I never listened to the teachers or anything. I was failing all my classes. I never did any of my homework. And then when I got up to junior high and got involved with chess, I started to play competitively in tournaments and going to Nationals. I started getting B's, then I started getting A's. I guess I would say that a lot of it had to do with chess in that

*it calmed me down, allowed me to focus, to pay atten-
tion in school.*

*I love the sheer competition of chess. You play
somebody you've never met; you don't know how good
they are. When you set up the board, you're both
equal. No matter if you're playing the number one
player in the world, at the beginning no one is winning, no one is losing. Everyone starts on the same
level. Once you start to play, each side can make mistakes, and then you win, lose, or draw. When you lose,
you just want to go over the game and find out what
you did wrong. When you win, especially at the Nationals, when you're sitting at the board for two or
three hours at a time and you're exhausted, but you
feel so good because you played your heart out, it's one
of the best feelings you could possibly have. After a
win, you feel great. Then I've won tournaments and
they called my name. You know, like "Chris Escobar.
Please come to the podium." All eyes are on you,
you're the best in the room, and you know no one
could beat you at that time.*

*I remember going to the park and playing guys
who had been playing for twenty years, and beating
them. People would hover around wondering who this
little kid was. That made me feel special, like "I'm
top-notch at this park." But then someone else would
come and whip me and get me off the board and say,
"Get outta here kid. Stop bugging me." That was cool.*

*I went to a junior high school called the Learning
Project on Twelfth Street in Manhattan. I wasn't the*

*best player on my team. I had to move on up. Our
school came out of nowhere, started busting up the top
teams in the city like Hunter. Still, the first time our
team competed at the J.H.S. Nationals was tough. I
actually wasn't supposed to go because we had a better
player. But we had a little tournament at the school
and I qualified as one of the top four.*

*We prepared hard for the Nationals. We would get
out of school at three-thirty and we would stay until
seven o'clock. We would play speed chess, going over
openings, going over middlegames, endgames, anything that would help us. We had a coach, Neil
Dorosin, who didn't get paid. He was a teacher at the
school. He didn't play chess real well, but he volunteered his time, after school, weekends, a lot of hours
spent to help us. Right now I can still talk to him
about anything.*

*The Nationals was exciting. After the last round,
we didn't know whether we were going to win or not.
We were hanging out in our room when our coach
came up and told us, "You guys won!" We flipped out,
started running around the hotel room. It had been so
much work, but it was worth it. The only sad part is
that the school had money problems and ended up
closing. We won the Nationals and now our school
doesn't even exist.*

*My mom passed away in my freshman year in high
school. I stopped doing anything, pretty much gave up
on everything, including chess. My aunt, who lives in
Miami, took me in. The change was good for me. I*

turned my grades around and got back into playing chess with my cousins. When I graduated from high school, I came back and CIS offered me a job. It's like a family here; they've known me for so long.

There are so many things I want to do. I love kids. I want to be a teacher, but I'm also interested in being a cop. I grew up in a tough neighborhood where cops were really rude, pulling over the kids all the time. I feel like maybe I can help change that by treating people better. But on top of that, I want to also own my business. The hours are long, but there's good money in it. This semester I took an intro business course.

When it comes to life in general, I try to think a couple of moves ahead. If it's going out with friends who might want to drink and drive, or just seeing the consequences of handing in a paper late. Chess is in every part of my life, at every level. It helps me relax, to take time out and go over stuff a couple of times. That helps you see all your mistakes.

If I was chancellor of the New York City Public Schools, I would implement chess in every school. I think chess would play a big role in kids' lives, and they would also get enjoyment out of it.

CIS now publishes their own materials with a curriculum for various levels of players. There is a rigorous training program for the approximately fifty instructors they send out every year. Educational administrators around the country call them frequently for guidance on how to replicate their success in other major cities.

Chess-in-the-Schools
520 Eighth Avenue, 2nd Floor
New York, NY 10018
Phone: 212–643–0225
Voice mail: 212–643–2947 and 212–643–3458
Fax: 212–564–3524
Web site: www.chessintheschools.org

♟ CHESS FOR SUCCESS (PORTLAND, OREGON)

When I was first invited to speak at the Chess for Success fund-raiser in 2003, I had frankly never heard of the program. The woman on the phone inviting me sounded lively and earnest, which made me feel excited about going almost immediately. When I finally met Julie Young, the foundation's executive director, I found her to be as pleasant in person as she was over the phone. A non–chess player herself, she extolled the benefits of the program to me as if I had never heard of the game. It's a phenomenon I find often repeated; once hooked, educators are ready to preach the virtues of the game to all ears.

I learned much about Chess for Success from Julie and the foundation's Web site. The program developed as an "outgrowth of the Portland Chess Project, an after-school chess program founded in 1992 . . . [and] launched in nine schools to see what effect chess might have on the academic performance, self-esteem and classroom behavior of students in the district's most disadvantaged schools."

The program only serves schools that qualify as Title I. Ninety-four percent of the children they serve have household incomes below 50 percent of the area median.

The project has mushroomed eightfold, going from two hundred kids to approximately sixteen hundred in forty-three schools since its inception. Asked the reason for their consistent growth in such a difficult environment, Julie quips, "Because the kids love chess."

Phil Margolin, the president of Chess for Success, is a true believer, especially because of the direct effect he says chess had on his own life. An acknowledged "bad student with a bad attitude" who flunked eighth-grade math, Margolin credits chess with turning around his grades and boosting his poor self-esteem. "I had to sit still, with my feet on the floor, and focus my attention on the board. I had to make decisions about competing good moves, and then reevaluate my decisions. I didn't realize it then, but I was developing the same skills children need to read a book with comprehension, solve a math problem, and take an exam. My grades improved, and so did my self-esteem. I went from nonacademic classes to the honors program. Today I'm a successful attorney and the author of ten *New York Times* best sellers. Not too bad for an eighth-grade flunky."

The thing that most excites Margolin is the cost-effectiveness of the program. "How can you beat seventy-five bucks a kid? Seventy-five bucks a kid! And we don't ask a dime from the schools. For something so powerful to be so cheap to deliver is just really amazing."

The proof in the pudding for any program is always the

effect it is having on kids. When I asked Julie to tell me a few stories, her voice took on a reverential tone, as if grateful to share something that has become her awe-inspiring responsibility:

> One of our great stories involves a little girl named Suzie.* I first met Suzie when I went to her school assembly to present a trophy to the chess club for their achievement at the regional chess tournament. The school borders a housing project and 80 percent of the children receive free breakfast and lunch. I sat in the audience next to Suzie, a painfully shy fourth grader. She was staring at the trophy and quietly asked me why I brought it to their assembly. I explained that it was for the chess club and then she asked me very quietly if she could get a trophy if she joined the chess club. I told her that many children win trophies, ribbons, and medals when they focus on learning and practicing their chess skills. She watched intently as the forty members of the chess club, all dressed in their blue chess club T-shirts, came forward to receive their trophy.
>
> The next time I saw Suzie was at the regional chess tournament the following year. Fifteen elementary teams competed to advance to the state chess tournament. Suzie had joined the club and worked hard to qualify for the team. She was beaming as she came

*Not her real name

up to the score table to announce her first win and I was surprised to see her shyness replaced with such confidence. As the day progressed, Suzie and her teammates advanced to first place and won a coveted place at the state competition.

The state competition had grown so large that it had to be held in two separate locations. I traveled back and forth throughout the day to meet with television and newspaper reporters. In the afternoon, I arrived at the elementary site and Suzie came running up to me with her arms outstretched and a smile that took my breath away. I asked how she was doing and she said, "I'm doing great." I asked how many games she won and she said, "Oh, I haven't won any games." She is a perfect example of what we try to teach the children—winning is fun, but it is not the most important part of chess. She was excited to be there with hundreds of children from all around our state. She made new friends and her team was being featured by one of the network television stations for the evening news.

Suzie's coach told me that she had a very difficult home life and that chess had turned her life around. She was self-confident, her grades and attendance had improved, and she was taking a leadership role in the chess club.

Several months later the Portland Trailblazers asked our organization to set up chessboards at one of the games and bring some children to play with the fans. I asked Suzie's team to come and they were thrilled. While the basketball game was going on, the children were able to go inside to watch. Suzie declined and wanted to stay with me at the chessboards. We talked about school and she told me about her cat. I asked if she had brothers or sisters. She said, "No, it's just my mom and me. My daddy left us one night without telling us where he was going and he never came back. He took all of my mother's money and the car. We found out later that he had a gambling problem. Then we found out that he had another family that he did the same thing to before he married my mother." I was stunned to hear her story and amazed at how chess had helped her overcome problems that had to be devastating for a child her age.

There was also a little boy named James.* James is a ten-year-old African-American chess player. His school is in one of Portland's roughest neighborhoods and 100 percent of the children in his school receive free lunch. James's chess club competed at the regional chess tournament and he played so well he advanced to the state championship.

He arrived at the competition with his father and two brothers, all dressed in black leather-like jackets. Throughout the day, the boys were very well-behaved and quiet. Their father offered to help me at the score table in the early afternoon. His speech was slightly

---

*Not his real name

slurred and the right side of his body was weakened
from childhood polio. He told me that people told him
that he would not have a normal childhood because of
his disability, but he learned to do everything with one
hand. He learned chess on a dare when a friend said
no way could he learn it. He taught his boys chess because he knew firsthand the benefits of the game. He
also taught them that they can do anything once they
set their minds to it, and not to let anyone tell them
otherwise.

Not long after James's father started helping me, he
looked up and said "I can't believe it!" It startled me
and I asked what he meant. He told me that his ex-
wife was in the audience and that this was the first
time she came to anything for the boys. I found out
later that he was raising the boys by himself in a one-
bedroom apartment and working as a caregiver at an
adult foster home. His commute takes one and a half
hours each way.

James had problems in school after his parents split
up six years earlier. His dad knew the value of using
chess to focus a child's attention and teach skills for
success in life, so he began playing chess with his boys
every night. Now James excels in school and wants to
be a lawyer because he talks a lot "and lawyers have to
talk a lot."

James took second place at the state championship,
beating children who were taught by a Russian grandmaster.

We also have a little girl, Karen, who's a member
of one of our elementary chess clubs. Karen has cerebral palsy. Her movements are erratic, she drools, and
she is confined to a wheelchair. One day the coach
paired Karen with one of the better players in the
club, a macho boy. He told the coach that he would
not play with her because she did not know how to
play chess well, but the coach suspected that the boy
did not want to play with Karen because she was a girl
and her disability makes her look odd. The coach told
him that it was not an option, so he sat down to play.
To the boy's surprise, Karen won. After the game, the
boy came up to the coach and in an awed tone of
voice said "Boy, she can play!" Within minutes chess
had cut across all barriers and eradicated differences.
That's the great thing about chess: Opponents are
equal at the start of the game.*

Chess for Success clubs are open to all children in the
school, bringing together boys and girls of all languages,
all intelligence levels, all ages, all socioeconomic groups,
and all ethnic groups.

Chess for Success
1030 NW 113th Avenue
Portland, OR 97229–5622

*Not her real name

Phone: 503–520–8960
Fax: 503–646–6004
E-mail: julie@chessforsuccess.org
Web site: www.chessforsuccess.org

♟ THE HILDA BLOWERS FOUNDATION (EAGAN, MINNESOTA)

Located in Eagan, a lovely city in southern Minnesota standing west of the Mississippi River, the HB Foundation is poised to become a prominent force in scholastic chess. As of this writing, the Foundation, which began in 1998, is set to announce a major new initiative: the sponsorship of the largest chess open tournament in history. The event is expected to attract worldwide attention and will likely shine a spotlight on the work that is the Foundation's stated mission: to develop critical thinking skills by introducing kids to the magic of chess.

Why would a foundation aimed at helping young people wish to sponsor a major international event? Executive director Brian Molohon explains: "We had struggled for a while to get people to realize that chess is more than a game, to find a way to break out of the box and to find a means of showing people that chess is not just another niche in the educational toolbox." After a good deal of discussion and analysis, the Foundation concluded that putting on the world's largest chess tournament would be a good way to accomplish that goal. "It would dramatically establish chess as a valuable educational experience, give it the exposure that it needs, and revolutionize the world of chess," said Molohon.

The normal duties of the nonprofit foundation are to initiate and support chess programs in the schools, to help support area tournaments and events, and to publicize the capacity of chess to improve cognitive abilities and critical thinking skills. "Our founder happened to hear you being interviewed on television about the work you were doing in Harlem, basically helping children break out of their surroundings using chess as a tool," Molohon said to me via phone. "Your words moved him to marry his vision of promoting education with chess. He was looking for a way to give back, so he said: 'Okay, there's a vision, let's combine the educational values of chess with the game itself and bring them together under the HB Foundation.'"

That decision led to the Foundation initiating chess programs in elementary, middle, and high schools all over the Greater Minneapolis community. The support includes paying for chess instructors, books, chess sets, and other chess equipment. Several scholarships have been doled out to students who maintain a high rating with the U.S. Chess Federation as well as excel in school. The Foundation has also sponsored several competitions, including the annual Check It Out tournament, which drew two hundred inner-city kids in 2003.

"We try to spread the word about chess," says Molohon. "I just hear all these stories about how chess changes lives. There are kids we support who are challenged with ADHD. Their teachers describe how they see the patience that chess develops, how it transfers to other subjects. There was a kid at St. Matthew's Catholic School named Eddie* who had all sorts of behavior issues, ADHD, family stuff. Since we started the chess program, he has just made an about-face. He has turned around in his attitude, in his schoolwork. He's become more cooperative with his teachers. And they don't tie it to anything but the chess program because they weren't doing any new interventions. When we introduced chess and they saw this pretty quick turnaround, they started to wonder what was going on.

"We have a neat program in Rochester, Minnesota, where we worked with an English as a Second Language program, where a teacher was using chess as a way to help kids learn English. Every day after lunch, the kids would play each other. The teacher would have them write down their notation, talk about their moves, and he would ask them questions. Imagine a classroom full of every ethnicity out there. One of the kids said that prior to the program they were the 'trash of the school.' Everybody looked down on them because they talked funny and dressed funny, just normal cruelty from kids. We went down there as a Foundation: We bought them memberships in the national federation and bought them equipment. They started to excel at the game. We got the radio and TV stations to come down and do a story on it. All of a sudden these kids became the leaders in the school. Other teach-

---

*Not his real name

ers would come to their classes and ask for these kids to be excused for half an hour so they could come in their classroom and teach their kids how to play the game. So here the game does all those cognitive things, but here it did a lot with self-esteem and leadership."

The Foundation plans to expand exponentially in the coming years, from supporting entire school districts to broadening their scholarship component to include kids all over the country.

HB Foundation
Brian J. Molohon, Executive Director
3140 Neil Armstrong Boulevard, Suite 311
Eagan, MN 55121
Phone: 651–209–3067
Fax: 651–287–0155
Web site: http://www.hbfoundation.org

My Students,
in Their Own Words

*If one is lucky, a solitary fantasy can totally transform one
million realities.*

—MAYA ANGELOU

It has been fifteen years since I first walked into a classroom, chessboard in hand, to teach a group of wide-eyed
elementary school kids how to play the game that is my
life. It seems funny now, but as I set up the black and
white plastic pieces and looked out over those bright curious faces, I saw myself as a revolutionary, a young Black
man who could change the entire way Black kids, and people, saw themselves, a notion that was only reinforced by
how quickly my students seemed to be engaged by my lessons. I was the most dangerous man in America; in my
hands was the secret of how to teach young African-American kids to think for themselves and to counteract the
negative stereotypes that threatened to sap them of their
intellectual self-esteem. With its exclusive focus on rigorous mental discipline, I dreamt that chess could break the

spell of athletic superstardom that had entranced so many ghetto kids. The kind of raw power the idea had over me was reinforced by the racist attitudes that I was bombarded with on a daily basis, where city cabs would zip by and storeowners would saunter close behind. As books like *The Bell Curve* sought to prove the inherent inferiority of people of color, I fervently felt that I had found the magical elixir that African Americans could use to prove to others that we were just as intelligent as anyone else.

Well, I can forgive myself now; after all, I was only twenty-three. Naturally, a monster as multitentacled as racism could never be brought down by a single bullet. But my naïveté was not entirely without value: It gave me a passion that went beyond the classroom. The extra time I spent working with my students after school, on weekends, and during the summer was fueled by my burning desire to make a monumental difference. Sometimes it pays to be young and idealistic.

Did my teaching chess to young people really change anything? The best proof is to hear from some of the kids I coached, the ones who are now adults capable of contemplating the effect chess had on their young minds. Their words are compelling testimony to the redemptive, uplifting power of chess. I was humbled to listen to them speak, to hear the once adolescent voices now deepened to a rich bass over the decade that had passed. I am impressed, proud, and grateful to have had any influence at all. Their poignant stories truly represent the triumph of the human spirit over seemingly overwhelming obstacles. And their lives—full, rich, and purposeful—reveal the force that a single idea can have when applied with fervor and love.

The vignettes that follow mainly relate the personal stories of the Raging Rooks. While I would go on to coach other teams to city, state, and other national titles, these young men constitute the first, and therefore oldest, group to whom I successfully taught chess. I've also included one story from my captain on another championship team, the Dark Knights, because his story adds a Latino perspective, further attesting to the universality of the game's influence. There were others I tried to get—in particular the first female captain of the team—but we were unable to connect for various reasons. I hope the narratives here will positively represent the broader spectrum of kids who came through my chess door.

Kasaun Henry, age 27

Captain, Raging Rooks chess team in 1991

Adam Clayton Powell Jr. Junior High School,
    J.H.S. 43

Place of birth: Harlem, New York

Education: Associate's degree in Liberal Arts from
    Borough of Manhattan Community College

Work: Music producer, chess instructor

Current activity: Pursuing a bachelor's in music at
    City College of New York where he is the recipient of the prestigious Mellon Mays award for
    postgraduate studies

I was one of five children. I had two sisters on my mother's side, and a brother and sister on my father's side. I didn't live with my father. I met him about three times in my life. The first time I was about eleven or twelve years old. He came by the house to speak to my mother. She called me into the room to talk to him. That meeting lasted about five or six minutes.

The neighborhood was rough, drugs on every corner. It was a funny situation: Anything could happen to an outsider, but once you knew certain people on the block, it was like a family. You were free from certain dangers. Still, you were not exempt from everything. There were shootouts where you might get caught up in the crossfire.

I was robbed once. I was bringing home money from packing bags and two guys saw me coming. One guy took me from behind, picked me up, and covered my eyes. He had me by my neck. The other guy put his hand in my pocket and took my money. So things could always happen; you know how it is.

One of my sisters who was twelve years older than I am got caught up with the drug scene, smoking crack, in and out of jail. She had six kids. My mother took care of them. Once, my sister chased me around the house because she wanted some change from me to buy drugs. I had to lock myself in one of the rooms and call my mother to resolve everything.

I learned to play chess in the sixth grade. The boys who knew how to play chess told me to get away from

*next to them because I was so bad. It's like I couldn't
be next to the high priest unless I was holy, unless I
was sanctified. I begged my mother to get me a chess
book. My first book was* Bobby Fischer Teaches
Chess. *In the parks in the neighborhood, if you played
chess well, everyone gave you respect. Even the thugs
respected guys using their minds playing chess.*

*I met a guy named Adam in 141st Street Park who
wanted to train me. I went to his apartment and he
sat me down at a table. He started talking very slowly
with a commanding, philosophical-type voice. He
said, "You are about to enter something which will
change your whole life." I thought, "Damn! Chess is
real." He showed me a* Chess Life *magazine and
talked about strategies, ideas, competition. He made
me want to be a warrior.*

*I remember meeting Michael [Johnson, future
teammate on the Raging Rooks]. He liked to play
stickball. He was the bully on the block and I was the
nerd. He saw me playing chess in the park and he told
me he would come by to beat me before he went
home. Then he came by and whipped my tail. I didn't
understand how he could beat me like that. I studied
hard, learned some things, and played him again in a
different park. We played this game and I was trying
to stop one of his pawns when he made a move that
shocked me. He did it so quickly, instantly. The idea
behind it was deep, but he had seen it long before. I
realized there and then that he knew something I
didn't.*

School wasn't hitting the right points. I had social problems. My character was different from the other kids. I had a strong religious background. I was ostracized because I didn't fit in. I didn't curse, I didn't get involved in certain activities. The problem with school is that the challenge is external, not internal. One of the hardest things to conquer is yourself. School did not nurse me the way chess did, in a way that could fulfill my potential. School feeds you knowledge, but school didn't help me deal with my problems in life. School didn't put me in contact with myself. I go to school and I'm doing something that gets on my nerves, then I still got to go back to the hood, and my family is struggling.

Being a part of the Raging Rooks chess team was like being a part of a family, a sense of camaraderie, students who shared the same passion. By studying with you, I knew I was good. You instilled a lot of confidence in me, and your lessons were phenomenal. I could actually feel the growth after each lesson. It was such a high, I forgot about everything. Chess changed my life. I was addicted to it, I went home and studied it, it made me feel better, I had a sense of purpose. Chess gave me a boost of confidence to be my own individual—it was my world, my thing. I was the one who won the games. It was my strength, and nobody could take that away. I became stronger as an individual, but more and more I repelled some of my friends. I remember a group of girls walked pass me at the bus stop and called me a nerd, but I didn't care because I was a good chess player. It would have been different if I was just a nerd. I was a part of a special team, I was traveling, and Maurice Ashley was my coach. I was doing my thing.

Winning chess tournaments triggered my life. I had the understanding that I could move forward, that I could do things, that I could be someone. It made me start to think that I had options, that I could pursue those options. I wasn't really aware of it at the time, but that was the beginning of a new way of thinking about life, that there was more than what I was seeing out there on the streets.

I became open to a lot of things. I fell in love with philosophy, languages. I was able to approach subjects in original ways. Chess can allow you to take ideas that don't seem connected and then make them come together down the line. Chess offers a complex way of thinking that unites a stream of melodies that don't seem to fit, makes them harmonious. Things can coexist peacefully even if they are independent. Sometimes I have to coexist with negativity. My sister's on drugs but I have to love her. She might rob me, but I have to live with her. Ultimately, that became who I am. That's me, that's my harmony.

Since I've been deeply studying music, I can see the many parallels between it and chess. In both, there has to be a stable idea, then the execution of it, then the need for harmony, and then the necessity for a proper tempo or rhythm at which you execute these ideas. Chess is a moving game. It's not stagnant, just like music. One of the most important elements of music is that it must move. It's filled with vibrations. These parallels give birth to other parallels: on how we create ideas, how we create moves, what it takes to improve. All these things are confluent. In chess, you have to get knowledge, you have to be creative with the knowledge, you have laws to learn, and you have to be ready for the exceptions. In music, it's the same. Plus, in both, each individual can play in their own way, they have their own voice.

Chess can be like jazz on the improvisational side, the spontaneity. Chess is like hip-hop because hip-hop vibes with a certain personality, goes its own way, like "This is how I get down." You can hear the voice of the chess player, like [former World Chess Champion] Tal doing his thing. Chess is also like classical music because it's all about structure, about order. There were times in classical music where people played a certain way, very dogmatic, but that had to evolve. The same thing happened in chess with Steinitz and Tarrasch bringing order to chess, too much order in fact, before the hyper-moderns turned the game around. Time periods represent the maturity of mankind, so music reflects that and even chess reflects that. Look at the effect of technology on chess.

Chess increased my concentration and focus. I developed that habit in a fun way. Chess showed me how to work hard, how to foresee the consequences of negative decisions. You become very scrupulous when you begin to play chess because chess is a dangerous game. It develops this way of thinking like let me watch out, let me analyze, let me be careful. This is natural in chess and in life. If someone tries to say something to you, your mind naturally tries to inquire about the veracity of what they're saying. Chess allows you to screen these things very quickly. Chess allows you to search for truth quickly; you learn how to zoom in.

Chess developed my character. Chess taught me morals, developed who I am. It taught me how to sacrifice. School didn't do that. I didn't care. When I was in high school, I didn't care. I was cutting class like whatever. School wasn't a nurturing environment at all. Chess brought me peace of mind and showed me who I am.

Now I know myself a bit better. In our day and age, guys on the street have no idea who they are. They are so consumed by the media, they're like drones. Now I love knowledge. When I first studied chess, hours were nothing. Days were nothing. It was just the joy for chess itself, a drive, a self-motivation. Even now, I'm trying to get back to that zone. I clearly remember how working hard at chess took me from one point to a higher one. I know I can be on point in my life because chess showed me the way. Chess ignited me. Someone lit a star that will keep burning as long as I live.

Francis Idehen, age 26

Member, Raging Rooks chess team in 1991

Adam Clayton Powell Jr. Junior High School,
   J.H.S. 43

Place of birth: Lagos, Nigeria

Education: Bachelor's in Economics, Yale 1999

Work: two and half years as a bond salesman at
   Goldman Sachs; three years as NASDAQ day
   trader; associate in JP Morgan's credit derivative's
   group

Current activity: enrolled in Harvard Business
   School

*I'm the oldest of five. I have two brothers and two
sisters. My family settled here from Nigeria when I
was nine. My father was studying medicine at the
University of Lagos, but my parents decided the kids
needed to have the best opportunity possible. Looking
back, it was a lot of foresight on his part to leave Nigeria. When we left, things were still kind of decent.
But from '89 to '97, no one wanted to be there. It was
just ugly, death, people were getting killed every day.
Sometimes people getting off the airplane would get
shot.*

*Being from Nigeria, I had to make a tough transi-
tion, trying to figure out how to exist in this country.
To be honest with you, seventh grade was a really tur-
bulent time for me socially. A lot of jokes from kids.
My family was dirt poor, five kids coming from Nigeria, moving to the States. I never had anything name-*

brand until I could afford it myself. You know how kids can be. They can be really superficial.

That might have been what attracted me to the chess guys. Maybe I felt more comfortable with that niche, that group of kids more so than the larger pool of kids that I was associated with. Also I talked differently, with my accent. Plus I spoke more properly so I was typecast as a nerdy kid. Kids treated us differently anyway just because we were in the SP class, so we were always called the nerdy kids. There were maybe two or three SP kids who happened to find the elusive balance between being cool and being smart. I just wanted to find a group of kids that I felt comfortable around. Kids in general never want to stick out. They always want to fit in and for me it was exacerbated because I was so different, I came from a different country, spoke differently, dressed differently. With girls especially, you just want to be cool.

I definitely got hooked on chess when I saw these guys go to Salt Lake City [Nationals, 1990]. I thought that this was the coolest stuff ever. The guys were getting to go travel to compete. I've always been competitive, athletically and academically. I fancied myself a basketball player, but the reality is that I was always more what one might call a nerd, I suppose. From a very young age I was always attracted to being able to travel. I just heard all these stories from the guys who went to the Nationals and I decided that I had to do it.

When I got good enough to be on the chess team, I felt really empowered. It was the first time I realized that you could come from nothing and become something. When I had gotten better, I realized that I had been an outsider looking in, then a year later I had made the team and even won a national championship. That made me feel like I was meant for more.

After my chess success, I felt different, especially by the time I got to high school and people got to hear of my accomplishments. It's funny. I think I felt like some of these athletes must feel when they achieve a certain level of excellence and prowess at their sport. You have a different swagger. Particularly after all the media exposure we got. Those limo rides to be interviewed by CBS hold such weight in my mind. Especially for a twelve-year-old kid from Harlem who's really from Nigeria.

My experiences with chess when I was so young influenced my chosen career path. For a little while, my pops wanted me to become a doctor. But the things that I chose to do were very analytical, high-pressured, intense. I think chess helped me learn the inner workings of any kind of warlike endeavor. I realize how much day trading (my first job) is an extension of chess. I very much view day trading, any trading, in the late nineties, when the market was very volatile, as a war, a battle. There's a lot of behind-the-scenes logistics that takes place, much like any military strategist would do, to trade a stock, to trade in the market or to sell bonds, or any kind of business endeavor where you are making evaluations based on how the market is performing and consequently making decisions based on that. Chess laid the foundation for me to that, to look ahead. I haven't played chess lately, I'm as rusty as ever, a scrub now, but I still have the skill of immediately looking ahead. I'm a dreamer, a risk-taker, but when I played chess I was not a risk-taker. Chess taught me how to balance that.

I think what chess has done for me is given me a lot of emotional intelligence and maturity. I realize a lot of times I feel like I see past what I'm being given on the surface, what is appearing to me on the surface in terms of, let's say, a conversation I'm having, or the way I'm being treated by someone or any interaction I have. I can see the underlying themes, what's really going on. I don't think I was born with that. It's something you come to when you learn how to analyze well. I just think the analytical benefits of chess are so abundant, so numerous, that you can't even quantify them.

I only realized all the lessons I learned from chess when I was twenty-four. Only then did I look back and see all the lessons I had learned.

Antonio Javier, age 25
Captain, Dark Knights chess team at Mott Hall, I.S.
   223, 1994
Place of birth: Santo Domingo, Dominican Republic
Education: Bachelor's in Economics, Cornell University, 2002; Master's in Public Policy, Cornell University, 2004

Current activity: spending a year in Japan to cement
    six years of Japanese study and find work in Japa-
    nese firm

*I was raised by my aunt. My birth mother allowed
her to take me from the Dominican Republic when I
was four. My aunt was what we call a* viajando, *someone who travels. She was one of the only people from
our family who was in the United States. Things were
tough back in Santo Domingo and I had a really bad
case of asthma, so my aunt decided to get me out of
there and my birth mother agreed that it was the right
thing to do. My birth mother finally came over about
ten years later.*

*We lived in Washington Heights. It's a mostly Do-
minican neighborhood. I was not allowed to go outside. It was always, get on the bus, go to school, come
right back. I've never been threatened or felt like I was
threatened, but there was always the drugs. There was
a fried chicken place on the corner and you just didn't
go in there because the drug dealers owned it. There
was a place my sister used to hang out called The
Block. A lot of dealers hung out there. She ended up
having a baby at sixteen by a guy who was a dealer.*

*Drug dealing was considered like a respectable
thing; these guys were making money, always coming
out with the latest sneakers. I remember people getting
killed in buildings. Murals would go up about people
who I used to see around [who got killed]. There's a*

corner that got painted over all the time with different murals.

A major part of what attracted me to chess was that it was something to do. There wasn't much to do at school other than school. At home there wasn't much to do either. When I started becoming involved in chess it was something that filled my life and ful-filled that thing that I was looking for, that something to do.

Kids treated us differently because of chess. I didn't feel any different from the other kids but there was definitely the nerd stereotype. Some of my friends were not treated that way; they managed to be popular any-way. But I wasn't affected by what kids said. We were representing the school, and I was captain of the chess team. Other kids' opinions were not that influential in stopping our team's development.

I don't exactly remember when I started getting good. But what I liked the most was going to tourna-ments on the weekends and competing with my friends. It was something where I had a lot of control. At home you get told to do stuff, and at school the same thing. When I was playing chess, I had this con-fidence that if I concentrated I was going to pull off something magical and win.

I still have that emotion when something in my life happens and I come up with a real creative solu-tion to something. I call it magical, like a chess tactic. You're looking at a situation and you think there's no way I'm gonna pull it off, or that there's no way it could happen. But then you sit back and think about it and come up with something. It's magical when it happens. It's like a lightbulb.

Chess gave me the ability to think ahead. But not just the raw ability to sit there and envision chess pieces on a board, but thinking about your life in general: academically, professionally, spiritually, or anything. Envisioning a goal and trying to see how you can get to that goal. And realizing that there's not only one way to get to that goal, that you have to see what kind of situation or environment you're in. I constantly find myself sitting back and thinking about what's the next move.

[Three of Antonio's teammates went on to New York University.]

Charu Robinson, age 26
Member, Raging Rooks chess team in 1991
Adam Clayton Powell Jr. Junior High School,
    J.H.S. 43
Place of birth: Harlem, New York
Education: Bachelor's in Criminology from John Jay
    University, 2003, after a couple of years at the
    University of Maryland
Work: coaching chess to inner-city kids

I've lived in Harlem all my life. I haven't seen too much upfront brutal violence, but I have a lot of friends who've been to jail, a couple of friends who've

*been killed. I've seen brains on the concrete, disgust-
ing stuff on the ground as I was walking up Lenox Avenue where someone had gotten shot. I've been around
a couple shootouts where I had to run. I've been ha-
rassed after school, kids trying to take your bus pass.
I've been pretty lucky. I've never been beat up, just
petty thievery like my hat's been taken, my bus pass
getting taken. I've seen my friends get jumped, fights,
people running with guns, typical hood stuff.*

*Growing up, I used to like school. It was so easy
that I really didn't have to work at it. We did the same
math from third grade to sixth grade, so I didn't learn
anything new. I messed up later by falling behind in
algebra because I thought it was always going to be
like that. Up to junior high school, I never really had
to work at school.*

*Although my father didn't live with me, he did
teach me how to play chess. I thought I was sharp before I got to [J.H.S.] 43. I never really lost to anyone
in chess, so I thought I was nice. Then I played a lot
of games at 43 and I kept getting mated really quickly.
I was eating chips and drinking sodas, and I would
just get mated in the middle of taking a sip. I was intellectual, but I was losing to street kids. A lot of the
kids in our school who played chess were thugs or popular. A lot of guys [who] were good in chess had street
credit. I got more nerd comments for getting good
grades than from playing chess.*

*For them chess went along with being dope with
street stuff like, "Oh, yeah, and I'll bust your ass in*

chess." There were mad thug kids that were nice, a lot of tough kids who were good in chess. I wasn't tough and they could beat me in chess so I was just like, "Damn!" It's like a nerd who gets jumped by a guy who gets better math scores.

I remember I couldn't even get on the team. But then I started beating some of the top players. I just shot up. I remember at the beginning of the year I wasn't even thinking about going to the Nationals. But then I moved up quickly and suddenly I was good enough to go to the Nationals. I started to understand that I had to protect my pieces and get [the other guy's] pieces. Then I became aware of avoiding sudden mates. I remember playing Mr. Gudonsky [science teacher] and he was pointing out all the things that were wrong with my position, like I was a practice dummy. We had the same number of pieces, but I had all these weaknesses, scattered pawns, and holes in my position. That's when I realized that there was more to the game than just the stuff each side had on the board.

We were glad to have you as a coach. You were this smart, cool Black guy who knew a lot about chess and knew how to relate. We had never come across a young Black man who knew that type of stuff. You spoke our language, you could understand what was wrong with us. It was like you were one of us, but you were nice in chess. Plus you crushed us so it was obvi-ous that you knew what you were talking about.

We used to look forward to what you were going to

show us. I remember you showed us some Morphy
game with some nasty mate with the two rooks. It was
like "Oh, snap!" It was then that I realized how grimy
it could be. When you go over games you made it seem
like the movies, like events. It was like you could
make people pay, that there was no limit to the
amount of pain you could deliver.

The only thing that used to get on my nerves was
when reporters asked me how it was that we won the
Nationals, like we were underdogs. They kept over-
playing how we were from Harlem. Yes, we came from
Harlem but we were prepared, we played all the time,
our coach was dedicated. We didn't even know it was
a big deal what we were doing coming from Harlem
until they were all over us like "How'd you do it?"
They acted like we were all failing out of school and
in juvenile homes. To me, we went to school, we liked
the games, we worked at it, we had good coaching,
good instruction. I mean, there were disadvantages,
like you might get jumped going home. But when it
came to the chessboard, that wasn't there.

It wasn't like someone was trying to stick you up
while you're playing the game. I could play 1.e4 [chess
notation describing the most popular first move] and I
knew how to develop my pieces, and if someone left a
piece unprotected, more likely than not I would take
it. I could checkmate with a queen and rook. The me-
dia acted like we were playing grandmasters. Why was
it so unbelievable that we were beating a bunch of B
and C players?

Chess gave me a chance to travel. I also got a scholarship to Dalton [an exclusive Manhattan private school] because of chess. I think I sealed the deal to get into the University of Maryland by putting the fact that I played chess on my résumé. Now I teach chess and make a living at it. I know a lot of the kids I teach enjoy it. I think being exposed to something else is good for them. I think it makes a difference in the kids who compete and win trophies. It gives them a lot of confidence.

Five

———

KEEPING

KIDS

INVOLVED

Twenty-five Activities to Keep It Fun

If your mind is empty, it is always ready for anything; it is open to everything. In the beginner's mind they are many possibilities, but in the expert's, there are few.

—SHUNRYU SUZUKI

This chapter discusses the many ways you can motivate your child to get more involved in chess. Let's face it: Not every child is going to want to take up the game right away. And even children who like chess might start to get bored with the same routine over and over again. In my classroom, I try any trick I can think of to keep my students perpetually stimulated. The suggestions below apply alternately to parents teaching at home and to coaches and educators teaching in school. Feel free to modify them according to your special situation. There are enough of them to keep the magic of chess alive for a long time to come.

♟ FOR YOUNGER CHILDREN (AGES 6–8)

1. Have your child draw and color chess pieces. Make a chess collage.

All young children love art. Drawing chess pieces is a great way for a child to express herself through the game. This is an especially good idea if, for one reason or another, the child is not really interested in playing right away. Art's noncompetitive nature appeals to kids who may initially be afraid to lose face by playing to win. This activity can then serve as a bridge to getting a child interested in playing an actual game.

Even if the child takes a great liking to chess, doing chess art can help stimulate some creative juices. *The Art of Chess* by Colleen Schafroth is a lovely book that has some wonderful pictures of beautiful chess sets. It could easily serve as a source of inspiration for children to do their own art, or maybe design their own chess sets for display. Interestingly enough, the great French painter Marcel Duchamp quit doing art in his later years to play chess full-time, rising to about the level of an Expert. He put it eloquently: "I am still a victim of chess. It has all the beauty of art—and much more. It cannot be commercialized. Chess is much purer than art in its social position."

Finally, any Internet search for chess art and figures will yield some nice images that can be printed out and used to make a collage. Check out http://www.chess graphics.net/ for some truly diverse artwork.

2. Make chess pieces out of Play-Doh or clay.

This idea is similar to the previous one, except here the child gets to create a set that she can use. Of course, whatever room this takes place in will be extremely messy until the set had been made. I apologize in advance!

Schafroth's book can also serve as an inspiration for this activity. There are no directions on how to make any of the sets included in the book, so I would be careful trying to do the more intricate ones. Young children might be a little sensitive if their pieces are not coming out quite right. If there are any such concerns, then suggest to the child that she make her own set that is loosely based on her favorite design.

3. Buy your child an exotic chess set like the Bart Simpson Set, the Superhero Set, or the Yankees vs. Mets set.

This is the probably the simplest way to get a child jumping up and down about playing chess. By combining chess with a favorite TV show, theme, or sports team, these sets motivate children to not only play chess, but also to play with the chess pieces themselves. Of course, they will be a little more expensive than a plain chess set, but it's worth it.

For those even more inclined, there are even fancier sets that might peak a child's interest but burn a hole in your wallet. Millions of kids worldwide saw the amazing giant chess set in the first Harry Potter movie with which Harry and his friends had to do battle. A smaller version of it is available (for about $350). Even fancier is the *Lord of the Rings* set, but this one is probably more appropriate for older children (and for those with $600 to spend). Check with the U.S. Chess Federation (USCF) at 800-388-KING (5464) for their various prices. You can also visit them online at http://www.uschess.org.

4. *Have a chess-theme party.*
Okay, this one is for the really adventurous. It's not every day that kids get to dress up as kings, queens, knights, rooks, bishops, and pawns. That means the entire project will have to be done from scratch, with the lucky leader of the group having to coordinate the whole thing. Well, who said enriching kids' lives was easy?

Of course, the kids will love it. They can create their own costumes from large cardboard boxes and good, old-fashioned watercolors. Punch some holes in the top of the boxes, tie on some strings and voilà! Naturally, there are costume stores that have medieval garb. One can also find loads of stuff on the Web. Check out http://hollywood-costumes.com/ for period pieces (and everything else, for that matter).

A real twist on this would be to use the original chess pieces, which, according to the best-known records, were Indian in origin. This means kids would come dressed as elephants, camels, horses, shahs, and viziers. The only problem here is that it might start to look more like an Aladdin-theme party.

The easiest part will undoubtedly be the pastries. Chess cakes and cookies are sure to go over big.

5. *Make up chess cards and play Chess Concentration.*
This is a twist on the classic children's game of Concentration where face-down cards are turned over two at a time to see if they match. It also has the benefit of combining an art project with a game the kids all know. Just have the kids cut out thirty-two rectangles from colored paper and then draw a complete set of chess men, making sure to color in the black pieces.

6. *Build chess towers with the pieces.*
The best pieces I have found are the classic Staunton pieces that can be purchased from the USCF. They stack up very nicely, so much so that it might be better to have two or three complete sets of pieces. It takes a steady hand, great concentration, and a lot of patience to do it right. But the young ones are often entranced watching and building them.

My personal favorite is to stack four rooks on top of each other, then add four knights in a circle onto to the top rook, and finally a queen on top of the four knights. What? You didn't think chess grandmasters would be caught dead doing something that silly? Then I guess you might laugh when you see me juggling chess pieces.

7. *Play Guess the Mystery Piece.*
A game of deduction. One side chooses a piece and hides it in his pocket. The other side gets three questions and three guesses to figure out which piece has been chosen. Once kids get the hang of this, then the more challenging version is to ask only two questions. Any question can be

asked (Is it a queen? Does it jump over pieces when it moves?). The trick is to ask questions that eliminate the other pieces from contention.

8. *Use chess pieces to make letter designs on the board.*
This is simple. Of course, many other designs are possible, such as numbers, geometric shapes, and logos.

♟ FOR EVERY AGE

9. *Play speed chess.*
For this, the kids will need a chess clock. What chess players call a clock is actually a device with two clock faces and two buttons on top. The basic rule for speed chess is that the clocks are set to five minutes per side. Each move must be followed by the moving side pressing the closest button. This stops one clock from running and starts the other. The players continue like this—move, press, move, press—until a clear winner emerges on the board, or one side runs out of time. Generally, the side that runs out of time immediately loses except in cases where the other side has insufficient mating material (a lone knight or bishop cannot checkmate a lone king by itself while a rook or queen can).

There are some who believe that speed chess is not a good thing for kids to play. They argue that chess is a thinking game, that the reduction of time retards the development of good thinking skills in young people. They even go so far as to say that speed chess could be potentially harmful to a young person's game, teaching them to be rash and impatient in an effort to win quickly.

I could not disagree more. I have worked with hundreds of kids in my career and I have found that speed chess actually *helps* build better thinking skills by forcing players to think faster and more efficiently. While it is true that the quality of the moves is not on the same level as the standard classic time control, the moves are good enough to make for interesting chess. A player must also develop other qualities in order to play speed chess well, qualities such as intuition, resourcefulness, and the ability to remain calm under pressure. There is nothing like a ticking clock to force you to think and act fast. I always made speed chess a part of the training of my three national championship teams; this training came in handy more than once.

It's important to note that this tool can also become very addictive. Most tournament players will not play casually without a clock, and will almost always play speed chess when they do. The key here is moderation. Like anything else, too much speed chess can work against you. Many park hustlers who gorge themselves on a steady diet of speed chess find that when they take their game to real tournaments, they don't hold up nearly as well. I have seen many park hustlers crush masters at speed chess, but fall apart against lower-rated class players in tournaments. They never learn that thinking quickly does not necessarily mean playing quickly in real competition. The lesson is to make sure that one does both; the benefits will be exponential.

Most chess stores still carry the analog clocks, but the digital clocks are more precise and have become much more popular in recent years. The USCF has all kinds, but an Internet search might yield a better price. Try www.cajunchess.com or www.wholesalechess.com for possible bargains.

10. Play Give-Away Chess.
The winner of this game is the one who can get rid of all his chess pieces. That's right: You intentionally place your pieces in harm's way so that the opponent can capture them. The idea is that whenever one side is able to capture one of the enemy's pieces, it must do so (the same as in checkers). If there is a choice of two pieces to capture, then it is up to the player to pick one. There are no checks or checkmates, and standard chess strategy gets thrown out the window. The bottom line is to have nothing left to play with. (Spend all your money since you can't take it with you.)

It sounds like this is certain to be counterproductive; why would anyone want to give away all the chess pieces? This one is a little tricky to explain, but I can vouch for its success. It builds visualization skills, and keeps chess light and fun. The game is stripped of all its complex strategic elements, and raw tactics take over. Kids who play this a lot come to quickly understand what the pieces can do, and how dangerous each move can be. And it's really great for when kids want to wind down.

11. *Play Chess Connect Four.*

This game is great for building coordination. Using a queen, two rooks, and a bishop, each player tries to connect the pieces on four contiguous squares (vertically, horizontal, or diagonally). One starting position is to place two rooks on diagonal corners and queens and bishops on center squares. The only rule is that all the pieces must move at least once before a winning position can be reached.

More difficult variants to this game are to play Connect Five (adding a knight) and Connect Six (adding a King). This really forces the players to enhance their coordination skills. In any variant, the initial position can be done at random. In other words, the players start with the pieces in hand and place them down one at a time wherever they want on the board. Once all the pieces are in the place, the game begins. Again, the sole limitation is that all the winning pieces must have moved at least once.

12. *Play The Invisible Pawn.*

One player mentally chooses a square on which stands an invisible pawn, and then writes down that square on a piece of paper. The other player places a queen on the chessboard and makes a move. If the queen has come closer to the square, the player says, "You're getting hotter." If not then, "You're getting colder." The side with the queen has ten attempts to zero in on the square, but must always move the queen like a queen. A variant to this game is to play with a rook, knight, or bishop.

13. *Hire a chess master for an hour.*
Call up your local chess club and find out if there are any masters or tournament-level players who would be willing to spend an hour showing your child(ren) some of the finer points of the game. Be sure to find out if the player has coached young children before. The chess master can also play a simultaneous exhibition (one player against many), or a blindfold game (yes, the player is blindfolded and calls out the moves). Any chess master will be able to do these activities, which will absolutely amaze both kids and adults.

It also might be intriguing to see if there are any really strong players who are of comparable age to your child(ren). Kids are amazed to see other kids who compete on the same level as adults.

14. *Visit the local chess club or park where chess is played.*
If you are fortunate enough to be in a city that has a chess club or park where people play chess, it might be a good idea to drop by for a visit. My students always loved these field trips. It gave them a chance to get out of school (always nice!), but it also let them see that we were not the only ones who played chess.

In the case of the chess club, it pays to call or even drop in for a visit before bringing the young ones. For the park, a scouting mission is definitely in order. The most famous chess-playing park in the world is undoubtedly Washington Square Park in New York City, which brings me to my next suggestion.

15. *Rent the movie* Searching for Bobby Fischer.

This is probably the most popular chess movie of all time, and is loved by kids and adults alike. It tells the tale of young Josh Waitzkin, a child chess prodigy who learns to play chess from a professional coach and from the street hustlers in Washington Square Park. The movie details his rise through the tournament ranks where he eventually competes for the title of National Elementary School Champion. This movie never misses, and it made young Josh into one of the biggest stars in the history of American chess. Its tale of young heroism usually motivates kids for weeks to come.

16. *Subscribe to* Chess Life *magazine.*

As children get a bit more serious about the game, it helps to get them reading more about the famous players. *Chess Life* is the national magazine of the USCF. The junior subscription rate as of this writing is $25 a year. (http://www.uschess.org)

17. *Play Random Chess.*

Players secretly set up the pieces in any way they want on the back row at the beginning of the game (the pawns are placed on the second row, as usual). Use a sheet of cardboard to hide what each player is doing. Once the pieces are set up, the board is removed and play begins. A variant of this is Super Random Chess. In Random Chess the players are limited to the first two ranks (rows). In Super Random Chess the players can use the first four rows.

18. Visit a children's chess tournament.
Call the USCF or your local chess club to find out if there are any local children's tournaments coming to your area anytime soon. For a child, there is nothing like seeing scores of other kids competing at an activity that she likes to do. Of course, the child might also decide on the basis of that visit that chess is not for her!

19. Visit kid-friendly chess sites on the Internet.
For links to a number of interesting Internet sites for kids visit http://www.vschess.org/kidszone/linkskids.htm. A more comprehensive list can be found in the appendix (see Internet Resources).

20. Find a chess pen pal for your child.
A great idea for classroom chess teachers. This is nothing more than for a child to be able to write to someone who has a shared interest. Names and numbers of chess clubs around the country can be found on the USCF's Web site at http://www.uschess.org and then clicking on "Clubs."

21. Buy a magnetic set for the refrigerator door.
Family members can take turns making moves daily until checkmate is achieved. This is great for getting the immediate and extended family involved. You might even want to bring guests in on the fun. Be careful that small kids do not play with these as they might be a choking hazard.

22. *Play Remove a Piece.*

Every five moves, the weaker player gets to remove a chess piece from the stronger player's board, starting with a pawn and working all the way up to a queen. This is ideal for when a young child really has no chance against Mom or Dad (which hopefully won't last long).

23. *Play team chess.*

Players team up to discuss (in hushed tones) and decide on moves. Although chess is often seen as a singular sport, the variant of team chess is an alternative that has been played for more than a century. The idea is that two heads are better than one. This is very rarely seen nowadays, but it could serve many purposes if done correctly.

For one, when players can talk to each other, ideas are exchanged that neither player might have come up with on her own. I would often put two players of very different strengths on the same team in order that the weaker player might learn from the stronger. This also had the effect of forcing the stronger player to articulate ideas that may have only been understood instinctively.

Another benefit is that the cooperative effort helps to build team cohesion. Players who may never have had a real reason to speak to each other are encouraged to try to work together. It's also a great way to break down the natural barrier of the sexes, as even in chess classes girls tend to hang with girls and boys tend to play with boys. And the fact that the teams could be switched around for a new game means that the class or team gets to know everyone else a bit better.

A variant of this game that is far more competitive and a lot less friendly is tandem chess. In this version, the teammates do not confer before each move, but instead play alternate moves in silence. This forces the partners to try to guess what is going on in each other's heads after every move. This is obviously much harder than regular team chess, and can be a source of consternation, especially for the younger players. I found that this game works best with teenagers of about even playing strength.

I would be remiss if I did not mention one of the most popular variants of chess among young players. It's called bughouse, and it is often played during downtime at most scholastic chess tournaments. It is infinitely more complicated than regular chess, and, as a result, very little by way of strategy has been agreed on. I remember thinking that I was a pretty decent bughouse player before meeting another group of bughouse maniacs who cracked up laughing at my opening moves.

The main idea of bughouse is that two teams of two players each play on two separate chessboards. The teammates must play white on one board and black on the other. Every time a capture is made on one board, that piece is passed over to the teammate on the other. The teammate is then able to place that piece down anywhere on the board when it is her turn to move. A board can look totally wild as positions with four white knights and twelve black pawns are not uncommon. Danger lurks around every corner since you never know when the opponent might get a monster piece that will land on the board and create havoc. Needless to say, bughouse is very addictive; coaches should be careful how they regulate it in class. But it is a great alternative to chess as it teaches tactics and teamwork. I personally enjoy it very much (although I played it much more when I was younger), and I always made sure that my students learned how to play.

24. Have the kids read chess literature.

No, not chess books meant to teach them about famous chess players and the nuances of the Najdorf Variation of the Sicilian Defense. I mean literature, stories that use chess as a theme. *The 64-Square Looking Glass,* edited by Burt Hochberg, is a great compendium of interesting chess stories. Unfortunately, most of the stories tend to be a little dark, and are more appropriate for the teenage reader. Other books along the same line include *Sinister Gambits,* edited by Richard Peyton, which has various stories with murder and madness as their themes, and the murder mystery *The Flander's Panel* by Arturo Perez-Reverte.

I would be remiss not to mention the instant classic *Searching for Bobby Fischer* by Fred Waitzkin. Yes, I did say to go see the movie. However, the book is absolutely fabulous, and should be read beforehand. Even readers as young as nine years old will enjoy this well-written book.

25. And finally, buy the CD-ROM Maurice Ashley
    Teaches Chess!

I don't mean to toot my own horn (well, maybe I do!). I designed this CD-ROM with the young chess player in mind. My first priority was to create an instructional CD that was also lots of fun. Although it came out in 1996, it is still timely and topical. Luckily, the rules of chess have not changed for over five hundred years!

I've listed twenty-five activities, but I can guarantee that there are scores more. I am sure another chess coach could add to my list in a heartbeat. Chess is so rich that there is tremendous room for creativity. That will forever be part of its magic and charm.

How to Keep
Girls Involved

Chess is as much a mystery as women.
—CECIL J. S. PURDY, INTERNATIONAL MASTER

Visitors to an adult chess tournament are often struck by the small number of female participants. While the U.S. Chess Federation estimates that women comprise approximately 8 percent of their adult membership, the percentage of women who actively compete on a consistent basis may be significantly less. A look at the list of the world's top one hundred players will reveal only one woman: the phenomenal Judit Polgar of Hungary. Why aren't there more women at top-level chess? This question has been the subject of speculation for decades, with answers varying from thoughtful to blatantly chauvinistic. It is not an easy question to ignore, since the women at the highest levels represent an important set of role models for young girls who aspire to play the game.

There are those who point to the small percentage of women in math, science, and engineering, and equate chess thinking with the thought processes one needs to excel in those fields. This argument is most often bolstered by studies that imply that men are superior at spatial activities while women are better at verbal ones. Other studies have suggested that the male brain tends toward specialization while the female brain is more balanced, with the masculine propensity toward obsession giving men an edge in fields where it pays to be focused and determined. These theories presume to be based on incontrovertible evidence, that men are indeed better at the activities in question. However, the lack of women in these areas suggests that the pool from which to draw conclusions is influenced by other pressures that have little to do with male superiority. Much like the early absence of Blacks in professional baseball had nothing to do with innate ability, the lack of women in chess is being strongly influenced by factors unrelated to a lack of specialized intelligence.

One would not know this listening to some male chess players. Grandmaster William Lombardy was quoted as saying, "Women play worse because they are more interested in men than in chess." In 1962, Bobby Fischer claimed that he "could give any woman in the world [the advantage of] a piece and a move"—meaning he could take off one of his pieces and allow her to move first. This handicap is so great that it would be plain suicide, as well as a deep insult, to try to play this way against a professional. Other high-ranking males have used a variety of explanations: poor physical endurance, insufficient aggressive tendencies, or the ultra-bizarre "lack of subconscious urge to kill their fathers." Even some female players have bought into the male superiority analysis, one going so far as to say that "We play worse because we are more tender, we have more feelings."

From my interviews with the current crop of skilled and influential female chess players, it seems the truth is as simple as it is complex. Beatriz Marinello, former women's champion of Chile and the current president of the board of the U.S. Chess Federation, points to the influence of stereotypical expectations. "I think my biggest obstacle was my father," she said. "At first he didn't mind, but when he saw how much I loved it and that I wanted to play all the time, he didn't like it that much. He thought that chess was not for girls." Susan Polgar, former women's world champion and the eldest of the three superstar sisters in chess, also emphasizes this social aspect: "[C]hess has been labeled worldwide as a boy's game. Until recently, girls were supposed to take ballet and music class, socially more feminine type activities."

Jennifer Shahade, 2004 U.S. Women's Champion, agrees: "Women don't get as much props at being good at independent endeavors. A girl is thought of as strange if she spends hours on end in her room studying something like chess. People are more apt to think that that's weird as opposed to ambitious or devoted."

The idea of chess being somehow unnatural for girls is not the only challenge these women have had to confront. There is also the issue of the fragile male ego. "In the beginning, the boys didn't want to play with me," says Marinello. "Some of them were embarrassed when we had tournaments and they found out they had to play me. They got teased by the other boys who started saying, 'You better not lose to a girl!' "

It's important to realize that this is in no way limited to chess; in fact, chess may be even more progressive than other competitive endeavors in allowing women to compete on equal terms with men. Golfer Vijay Singh's retrograde reaction when the number one female golfer in the world, Annika Sorenstam, first expressed her desire to play in a men's tournament is just one example of how a woman trying to compete with men is often pressured to stay in her place. The criticisms did not deter Sorenstam from playing, and she went on to finish ahead of almost half the field. Later she admitted that it was the most difficult experience of her life as she felt as though she was shouldering the burden of her entire gender. If a world-class competitor can feel this degree of pressure and discomfort, one can easily imagine why so many young girls shy away from fields that have been almost exclusively the domain of men. It takes an extremely strong personality to go where one is viewed as different.

In addition to dealing with the sensitive self-esteem of men, Polgar noted another, more universal, issue. "There's . . . the problem, that's not just in the chess world, of [a girl] being looked at as a sexual object, a girl all surrounded by guys. It's often a competition between the guys to see who succeeds with her. Obviously there are some girls who like that attention, but many girls quit because they get uncomfortable in that environment where they are singled out not for their chess game, even if they play well. It's not a healthy situation all around."

The boys-as-winners, girls-as-the-spoils mentality seems exacerbated by images propagated by society over the centuries. "Generally, in sports and other competitive endeavors, boys are encouraged more and have more role models," says Shahade. "You turn on the TV and the famous males are sports stars and politicians, and for women, the most prominent role model is Britney Spears." This attitude quickly filters down to young kids. "I was a fairly smart girl," says Marinello. "Boys don't like smart girls as much as they like pretty girls. But also the girls don't like you to be too smart either. It's always an issue there, when you are better in some ways."

With such a powerful bias working against them, these women were able to excel for various reasons. In the case of both Polgar and Shahade, they had the support of their fathers from the very beginning. Marinello points to her "stubbornness" and the special feeling that chess gave her, that she had somehow found her niche. When asked what they thought were the best ways to motivate girls to play chess, the answers fell into four categories:

1. **Strong family support:** It pays to have parents, educators, and coaches who look at young girls, and women in general, as real competitors. Also, parents who are willing to step outside the box provide excellent psychological and emotional support to their girls in the long run. "My family

has always valued things like creativity more than toeing the line," says Shahade. "I never thought it was bad that I was doing something [that others thought] a little eccentric."

2. **Find female chess mates:** If at all possible, finding and encouraging other girls to play will make a girl feel less isolated. All-girl teams as well as special training directed to girls' groups seem to make a difference. Even if it's only for a short time, it gives the girls a strong initial sense of camaraderie that may sustain their interest in the long run. Marinello's own personal experience is telling: "The first time I went to a chess club, I was thirteen years old. I saw only men, particularly old men, and it was scary. I didn't want to stay. But luckily there was another girl there that day in the same situation and the manager arranged a game between the two of us. Eventually the two of us became the two best female players in the country. If she hadn't been there that day, maybe I never would have gone back."

3. **Start young:** Girls are typically just as enthusiastic about learning chess in elementary school, a time when the pressure for males and females to separate into gender groups is not as pronounced as in later years. However, the onset of puberty changes the dynamics. "Between sixth and eighth grades, I was a little too young to be hanging out with boys," says Shahade. "So I didn't have any-

body to have fun with at tournaments. I stopped playing during those years and didn't come back until high school." While parents can help keep outside social forces from stopping girls from playing chess, it's much easier to do so if their girls have been playing since they were four or five years old. By the time they get older, the game will have become such a part of their sense of identity that they will be far more inclined to stick with it later on.

4. **Identify role models:** With the almost complete absence of intellectual women on television, it's important that parents seek out books and articles that showcase women who excel in scholarly fields. "My mother, Sally Solomon, really helped a lot," says Shahade. "She was a decent chess player, but she was extremely ambitious, and it helped develop my ambitious character. She's a professor at Drexel University; she's also into games like poker and bridge. She's always doing a million things."

In an age when women are more glorified than ever for being sexual objects, it is a challenge to get young girls excited about typically older brainy women. This needs to start at a very young age so as to provide some buffer against the inevitable flood of images to which girls will later be exposed by the mass media. (Interested parents can get a wealth of information on girl-

friendly resources at the Web site for girls at
http://research.umbc.edu/~korenman/wmst/links_
girls. html.)

Since Judit Polgar has already risen to the number
eight slot, the question of a woman being capable of playing with the men seems already answered. The thornier
issue is whether society will ever progress to the point
where a woman competing on equal terms with men is
not seen as a threat to the dominant male establishment.
It is not a problem that will disappear overnight; the struggle for equal gender treatment continues to be fought at
many levels. But thanks to Polgar, Shahade, Marinello,
and others, the chessboard has the potential to become
the new battleground for the minds of millions of little
girls.

For more on these women consider the following:

Susan Polgar: author (with Paul Truong) of *A
World Champion's Guide to Chess* (Random
House). Visit her Web site at http://susanpolgar.
com/polgarchess/index_polgarfound.jsp
Jennifer Shahade: author of *Chess Bitch: Women
in the Ultimate Intellectual Sport* (Siles)
Beatriz Marinello: Visit her organization's Web
site at http://www.uschess.org.

Six

A

FEW

LIFE

LESSONS

We can be so overwhelmed by detail and complexity that we become unable to abstract the underlying meaning of a situation.

—FROM *SEVEN LIFE LESSONS OF CHAOS*
BY JOHN BRIGGS AND F. DAVID PEAT

There are a number of lessons that I tried to pass on to my students. Many of them pertained to tactics and strategy, endgame technique, and opening insights. However, the best lessons I imparted had less to do with the nuances of chess, and more to do with the game's connection to life and life's connection to the game. None of these lessons were brand new; the great philosophers and sportsmen had spent years of concentrated thought and practice discovering them.

For me, it was the medium through which I came to deeply appreciate these truths that mattered. Chess cemented these ideas onto my being, allowing me to understand them with a special flavor peculiar to chess itself and then to try to pass them on to my students. This revelatory quality to chess allows it to truly shine as a teaching tool. That the game can be used to better understand some of life's processes attests to its profundity. Below I share a few thoughts on four of the lessons I've learned. I could have kept going, but that's another book unto itself.

♟ EMBRACE CHAOS

The unpredictable nature of chaos is one of our biggest fears. We attempt to live carefully ordered lives in the hopes of avoiding the confusion and disarray that a lack of control might engender. Unfortunately, as the evening news dramatically confirms, it is an impossible task. Stuff happens. Tornadoes, fires, car crashes, killer snowstorms—the list is endless. Less traumatic but still stressful are a litany of normal life changes: the move to a new city, changing jobs, the first day at a new school, the experience of a divorce. All of us, at one time or another, have found or will find ourselves caught up in a wave of bedlam and uncertainty. It's simply the way of the world.

In chess, players try to avoid these chaotic situations like the plague. As if maneuvering a ship through twenty-foot swells, we cling to well-known strategic principles in the hopes that they will guide us safely to shore. Unfortunately, the infinite complexity of the game often mocks our puny efforts. The endless possibilities—numbering into the billions after just the first four moves—often produce situations where even the best chess players face confusion and panic. The more the mind tries to impose logic and order, the more slippery and frustratingly defiant the position becomes. I know of one grandmaster who will sit like a deer caught by headlights as the waves of variations crash over his mind. Often, in his daze, he won't realize that his allotted time has run out. Long after the game, he's often seen walking around with the same look of confusion on his face. His is a classic case of chaotic paralysis. We have all been there.

"Chaos is nature's creativity." So says John Briggs and F. David Peat in their illuminating book *Seven Life Lessons of Chaos*. They write that we are so often wedded to our own ideas about the world that we stick to them no matter what the situation, creating a "negative feedback loop." Chaos helps us to break free of the loop, to see the world in a fresh creative way. We are forced out of our routine and into a new way of thinking. It's not that our principles are no good; they simply do not fully embrace this new setting. Often it will be a combination of the old principle and a subtle nuance that merge to create a brilliant nexus of thought, an innovative idea that fits the situation better than anything before it. As long as we remain open to the possibilities, we need not be overwhelmed by the craziness. We can simply accept that the moment is here to teach us something new that we could not have learned from riding the same bus every day. We need to be ready to act without the numbing fear of making mistakes; even those mistakes are part of the canvas.

How we handle chaos may say more about our intestinal fortitude than anything else. There are some grandmasters who relish bedlam, even making a conscious effort to engender it. Former world champion Mikhail Tal lived for turmoil and confusion. He was once quoted as saying, "You must take your opponent into a deep dark forest where 2 + 2 = 5, and the path out is only wide enough for one." He knew full well that the natural reaction is panic or breakdown. Still others respond with varied emotions: fear, anger, confusion, denial. All of these responses are natural.

What I've learned from my chess training is that it is possible to work with chaos, to ask it to show you the way forward. No matter how crazy the situation, it helps to do a few things:

Check out your own feelings. Address them first, if you can, before addressing the problem. Laugh at yourself. Movie director Stanley Kubrick's comment about chess feelings could easily apply to chaotic situations: "You sit at the board and suddenly your heart leaps. Your hand trembles to pick up the piece and move it. But what chess teaches you is that you must sit there calmly and think about whether it's really a good idea and whether there are other, better ideas." In key crisis moments during chess games, I will get up, walk around, and remind myself to focus on the moment. This usually brings greater clarity and allows me to focus on the business at hand.

Accept that there are no perfect solutions or mistakes. People often get bogged down in the flaws of each approach. What they don't realize is that everything is magnified under chaotic conditions because the charged emotional content makes things look bigger than they are. Grandmaster Savielly Tartakower made this point: "Some part of a mistake is always correct." Even when we are wrong, there are valuable lessons to learn for the next time we face the same problem.

Prepare for chaos. Many people assume that when something crazy happens they will just handle it. Unfortunately, when the situation begins to spiral out of control, they realize that they are completely unprepared to deal with it. It's incredibly useful to develop a set of responses to crazy situations beforehand, whether it be a fire, a criminal act, or an aggressive driver cutting you off in traffic. Not everything can be anticipated precisely, nor does it need to be. Just training oneself to get into the right frame of mind can be of huge benefit when the moment calls for it.

When something unforeseen happens to me during a game, I sometimes tell myself that I am going to lose. Much of the tension is quickly released from my body because I know from experience that losing is not going to wreck me. In that more relaxed state I can then deal with the problem on face value instead of blowing it out of proportion. This kind of reverse psychology on oneself may not work for everyone; the key is to find one's own preset method for dealing with the unexpected twists of life.

Act. If the situation is truly chaotic, it is sometimes impossible for thinking to reveal the exact solution. In such circumstances, it is important to test the waters by trying a path that looks reasonable without totally committing oneself. You might burn up some resources, or not pursue the optimal direction, but you don't waste time sitting still.

Chess players are usually afraid to do this because of the deep fear of making a mistake that the other player will exploit. They should take heart in the words of the legendary Mikhail Tal: "Later, I began to succeed in decisive games. Perhaps because I realized a very simple truth: Not only was I worried, but also my opponent." Everyone worries, even the brave. Training ourselves to act despite fear is the greatest lesson of all.

♟ USE AGGRESSION TO YOUR ADVANTAGE

In this society, we tend to worship aggression. We like our football teams to overwhelm the other team with power and brute strength; our basketball teams to dunk early, often, and with ferocity; and our action heroes to annihilate the villains, preferably with explosive firepower. While baseball might bring us subtle victories—a walk followed by a steal, a sacrifice bunt to get the runner to third, and a fly ball to get the runner home—we know full well that "Chicks dig the long ball."

Sports pages are filled with words like "punishing," "explosive," "crushing," "dominant." The popularity of WWF wrestling is probably not for the nuanced application of expert technique. "Pound 'em into submission" is more like it.

Teams are taught to be aggressive, even on defense. The 2004 NBA playoffs saw the Detroit Pistons attack without the ball, flustering opponents with twenty-four seconds of crazed, in-your-face belligerence. The other teams had a hard enough time staying in their shorts much less holding on to the basketball. Great football linebackers all share this mad-dog approach: Teams seemed overly concerned with stopping former New York Giants great Lawrence Taylor, who was so ferocious that teams would send two of their players to guard him and keep him from wreaking havoc around, near, or on top of their quarterbacks.

In chess, attackers like Kasparov and Tal sweep through their opponent's forces like a Category 5 hurricane. This kind of aggressive behavior is plain fun to watch, as long as it's in a controlled setting and produces no real victims. And as long as it's not directed at us.

I was a champion of the aggressive style for most of my career. Early on, my strategy mainly consisted of marshaling my forces, taking aim at the enemy king, and blasting away. That worked for a long time, especially since I had the unusual ability to judge when I could give away a pawn or two to generate the momentum I needed to launch the rest of my forces at the enemy king. The strategy worked with ruthless efficiency; I would go long stretches without losing a single game to masters and experts.

It wasn't until my opposition stiffened at the international level that I realized I had to change my approach. Blows that used to knock out unsuspecting victims now landed like tired jabs in the twelfth round of a boxing match. Grandmasters would take my pawns, defend carefully for a few moves, and slip into the holes left behind by my attacking forces. One player was kind enough to tell me that my style was superficial, based on tricks. I say kind because criticism, no matter how much it hurt, always helped me in the end. I just had to figure out what to do about it.

The solution came in the unlikeliest of places: the martial arts. My friends and I were all karate junkies; we would spend hours watching badly dubbed Chinese movies. I never missed an episode of David Carradine in the popular TV series *Kung Fu,* where the star would call upon his training as a young Shaolin monk to deal with everyday challenges. His memories of his master's sayings, always beginning with his nickname Grasshopper, were simultaneously profound and befuddling:

"Act like this candle."

"Become one with the river."

"In order to grab this pebble from my hand, you must stop wanting to grab the pebble from my hand."

With most of those statements, I appreciated that they reflected deep truths without having a clue as to what they meant. But somehow it would tie into the show neatly with a nice fight scene to end it all off.

The revelation connecting chess, the martial arts, and aggression came to me in the fall of 1997 after I had been to a chess tournament in Budapest. Even though I was now an international master, I was still plagued by my old super-aggressive solution to everything. I ended up losing several games and went back home in a funk. Days later, when I was studying my games from the tournament, an idea coalesced in my mind. I began to see beyond the idea that it was my premature attacks that were losing me games: I now saw that the *fact* that I was attacking caused most of my problems. I was constantly trying to impose my will (wanting to grab the pebble) instead of playing what the situation on the chessboard demanded (become one with the river).

Top athletes understand this principle quite well. I remember a Kobe Bryant quote about his radically different performances in the first and second half of a basketball game: "I was trying to force it at first. But coach talked to me about it at halftime, and I just came out and let the game come to me."

My chess game changed dramatically when I stopped forcing things. Before, I was afraid that if I let the opponent attack, I might be crushed myself. I soon realized the opposite: By allowing an attack I could use the energy projected at me to make my counterattack even stronger. The popular martial arts of tai chi and aikido are built on this principle. I even took up the latter to better appreciate the concept on which it was built. The idea, I learned, was similar to a boxing match when one fighter throws a hard punch. If it lands, great. But a miss exposes the ribs the punching arm once covered. In addition, it takes a moment to get back on a balance, time the opponent can use to land a crushing blow of his own.

One may wonder how this relates to chess, but the connection is not much of a leap. The chess forces act best when they are a coordinated unit, working as one toward the common goal of checkmating the king. In this way, they act much like the human body where even a slight push can cause us to lose our balance. In chess, if one piece decides to pursue an alluring attack at the price of unity with the rest of the forces, it will usually fail, and this failure will take its toll on the game as a whole.

It's a fairly easy concept to understand, but it took some time for me to comfortably incorporate my new understanding into my play. Soon, I was defeating players I had never defeated before. In one very important game, I defeated the reigning U.S. champion Larry Christiansen by mostly using his own ideas against him. Instead of thinking about how to defeat him with sheer power, I studied each one of his aggressive moves for any small weakness. It's incredibly frustrating to play against an opponent who neither attacks nor defends, who simply points out the flaws of one's moves. In the end, he made an aggressive mistake that cost him the game and allowed me to qualify as the first African American in the 157-year history of the U.S. championships.

My relationship with aggression continues to evolve. Now I welcome aggression as a test of my own mental balance. I still struggle to know what it means to bend like a willow in the midst of a pounding hurricane, or to relax when rip tides threaten to pull me under. There are even times when I can't help myself, and I play my old attacking brand of chess just for the fun of it. I win some, and lose some. Old habits die hard. Invariably, by facing—and practicing—aggression, I learn a little bit more about myself under pressure. And I've replaced the awe that aggression engenders with respect for its power. There is a time and place for everything.

♟ GET GOOD TO REALLY APPRECIATE GREATNESS IN OTHERS

One of the great benefits of being a grandmaster is that it allows me to really appreciate how hard it is to be good at anything. The field may vary: sports, entertainment, law, medicine, farming, pottery. Whatever the endeavor, the top performers are those willing to invest in the hard work, dedication, sacrifices, and long hours of study and practice that separate them from the rest.

When I met with Wynton Marsalis, a chess fan, at his apartment near Jazz at Lincoln Center, he made this point clear: "I would not deign to play you. I'm nobody. I know what kind of shedding [hard work] it took for you to get good. I'd feel like I was wasting your time."

Coming from conceivably the greatest jazz mind of the last twenty years, this might seem like a strange amount of humility. But it is actually the reverse: It is his enormous self-confidence in his own abilities that allows him to fully understand the true depth of skill required to be a master of a craft.

Of course, the same thing happens within fields all the time. Salieri could deeply feel Mozart's brilliance because he had achieved an amazingly high standard himself. In many ways, only basketball players can truly appreciate what it took to be Magic Johnson or Michael Jordan. My students used to wonder how anyone could beat me; my telling them that there were other players better than I was in all aspects of the game always drew disbelieving stares. Only when a few of them reached the Expert level did they begin to realize some of the finer distinctions. I believe it was my student Charu who said, "As I got better overall, I realized just how hard it is. It was like I was getting worse because I was getting better."

The world's best female player, Judit Polgar, opened my eyes to this on another occasion. At the time she had already been an acknowledged chess superstar, having crushed grandmaster after grandmaster with her brand of bruising demolition chess. Her nimble capacity for seeing hidden moves and springing them on unsuspecting opponents had elevated her into the ranks of the world's top twenty players. I was a big fan and had managed to make her acquaintance when I was an international master. Seeing how she was having trouble against the top four or five players, I asked her this question: "How do you get past the level that separates you from the very top?"

She paused for an instant before correcting me: "You mean levels." I knew that she was a better player than I was, but that slight adjustment made it clear to me that the gulf between us was even wider than I had suspected. In an instant, I felt my mind stretch at the implication: She could see what I could not. While I could see that she lost to the likes of Kasparov and Vladimir Kramnik, she could see *why and by how much.* I imagined it was like climbing Mount Everest: The higher one goes, the harder it becomes to go higher. It's called rarified air for a reason.

Those who have achieved excellence in one field are far less likely to criticize performers in others. Call it professional respect: It's just too hard to get good at any one thing. That is why I recommend to everyone that they try to get really good at a craft. Doing this allows you to see the world in a very different way. You begin to realize what real quality is and what it really takes to get there. The humility and self-confidence gained is awe-inspiring.

♟ TO GET BETTER, BECOME LIKE A CHILD

In early November of 1997, I wrote this note to myself:

> *Today I saw a knight again for the first time. I did not know it could do so much! Actually this all started yesterday as I was stunned by the war that a knight could have against two connected passed pawns. It continued today when I studied how easily a knight could be trapped by an opposing king and knight. To think that such simple mysteries are still present on the chessboard stuns me. What game have I been playing for the last seventeen years?*

Reading these words so many years later fills me with a twinge of jealousy. It was a mind-set that allowed me to make a dramatic leap forward as a chess player, just prior to completing the second stage of the grandmaster title. I can only vaguely recall the state of mind I was in, the feeling of seeing everything through a beginner's eyes. The chessboard often inspires that kind of awe, but only when you are ready to receive it. The feeling of wonder releases the mind and prepares it for a higher level of awareness. It's no accident that I played some of the best chess of my life around this time.

Professionals of all stripes often become jaded; winning often dominates learning and growing. I've seen it many times in the eyes of my colleagues; when you know too much, the thrill and amazement felt in the early stages just don't occur as frequently. It's as if knowing too much is a curse, making everything seem wooden and predictable. Without the possibility of surprise, enthusiasm often wanes.

When I need a shot of awe, I go play with my son Jayden. At two, the whole planet is a mystery to him. He is the perfect replica of his big sister, Nia, who, when she was two, would hug a tree as if it were a long-lost friend. When my son yells "Train!" you would think that a tornado had suddenly formed in the clear blue sky. A similar thing happens with planes, ants, bugs, dogs, cats, and the garden hose. I am reminded of a biblical scripture that says something to the effect of "You must become like a child to enter into the kingdom of heaven." Seeing Jayden squeal in delight at his mother playing peek-a-boo in plain sight makes me wonder if heaven could give more ecstasy than this.

I often leave the chessboard alone for weeks. When I return, the pieces look like alien artifacts. I feel a twinge of excitement, as if I'm about to flirt with a beautiful stranger. The chessboard welcomes me back: It will smile at first, play coy, make me feel uncomfortable with uncertainty. Then suddenly it will open up and reveal a shining mystery, so bright that it amazes and astonishes me. I'll sit in shock for a long time before the giddiness of youthful delight overcomes me. Soon, I'll be divulging the secret to my chess buddies, and they, too, will be stunned. Then we'll laugh, like children, and wonder what game we've been playing all these years.

MORE

TIPS

AND

TOOLS

A. FAQS TO GETTING STARTED FOR PARENTS AND EDUCATORS

For Parents

1. How old should my child be to begin playing chess?

A normal age to begin teaching a child is five or six. However, some children may be ready to start as early as four, sometimes even three. The key is not to force your child to learn; sometimes the youngster may just not want to do it, for various reasons. You can always come back to the game in six months to see if your child is ready and interested.

2. Should I teach my child myself?

If you think you are able, then it's a great idea to interact with your child this way. Parents know their children best and are able to tell when their child is getting tired, bored, overloaded, or uninterested. The only problem arises when a parent doesn't know all the rules of the game or has learned the rules inaccurately. The best way to guard against this is to purchase a good beginner's book, like *The Complete Idiot's Guide to Chess,* by Patrick Wolff, to get a thorough grounding in the basics.

3. How can I help my child if I do not know how to play?

Learn to play! But if you just don't have the time or you are feeling too intimidated, then ask around. There is bound to be a family member, a teacher at school, a class-mate, or a friend who knows the basics and would be will-ing to teach your child. The major warning here is that many people who think they know how to play do not know all the rules or some of the basic strategies. The two key questions to ask are "Have you ever read a chess book?" and "Have you ever played in a chess tournament?" If the answer to both questions is no, then be skeptical. This person might inadvertently impart the wrong infor-mation to your child. If the person has only read a book, that's just fine. He or she can provide a very nice start. If you meet up with a tournament player, you've struck gold. You can rest assured that most everything your child hears will be useful and thorough.

4. Is a coach useful for my beginning child?

It depends on the level of coach. For a child who is just starting out, I usually encourage parents to get a nice ba-sic book for you and/or your child to study from (*Bobby Fischer Teaches Chess* works for both parents and chil-dren). A coach can be expensive (from $25 to $200 an hour), and it is a relative waste to spend this money to teach your child the very basics. Quality books, good software, and videos can get your child started on the fundamentals. Once your child is really showing an interest and would like to get better quickly, then getting a coach is not a bad idea.

5. What are the traits of a good coach?

As with any teacher, a great coach is ultra-patient with his or her students. If your coach seems overeager and promises to make your child into the next Bobby Fischer, look out. If a coach insists that progress takes time and depends on the hard work of your child, then you have a winner.

Watch out for coaches who want your child to memorize lots of opening moves. The accepted way to teach chess strategy is to begin with the basic endgames first and then the tactics of middlegame, paying only modest attention to the opening stages. Coaches who try to switch the order do not understand how chess learning best proceeds and develops.

6. How many hours a day should my child practice chess?

After schoolwork and regular exercise (a healthy body makes for a sharp mind), your child might want to spend thirty minutes to three hours a day playing. Naturally, like anything else, the more chess games your child plays, the better he or she will become. However, simply playing is not the best way to improve; practice must be complemented by study. Whether it's chess books or instructional software, a daily program of concentrated learning will take a child much further than his or her peers who only play. My suggestion: For new players who fall in love with the game, play as often and as much as possible for the first couple of months. Once your child seems serious about playing, then introduce him to the magic of the game with basic books (see Recommended Books).

7. My child does not seem to like chess. What can I do to motivate him?

Read the section in Chapter 5 entitled "Twenty-Five Activities to Keep It Fun." There should be something in there that your child will find interesting. If your child simply does not want to do anything, then try to find the root cause of the reaction. It may simply be lack of readiness to learn to play, which is easily fixed by waiting a few months. You could also leave the chess set in plain sight in the family room or play a few times with a friend when your child is around. If your child is completely uninterested in learning anything at all about chess, do not force him. There is no doubt another amazing activity that your child is destined to do.

8. I am a much better player than my child, and he feels awful when he loses to me. Should I let him win?

The answer to this question depends on your personality and your child's intuition. My preference is to try to find players who are on the same skill level as your child. I never felt right allowing a child to beat me, because it seemed unearned and because other kids might suspect that it happened and discredit the kid. However, in my case, I was already a top player when I started teaching. I am aware of the other argument that beating an adult is a surefire way to build confidence and self-esteem in a child. While my belief is that there are other superior ways to boost a child's ego, it's hard for me to refute the potential gains of that way of thinking. My best advice is to use your discretion, but be wary of the consequences of throwing a game to your child.

9. Should I allow my child to play against adults in the beginning?

In chess, age is not a sure measure of ability. Children love to compete on equal terms with adults, and chess is one of the few places in life where a young child could potentially beat an adult pretty easily. If your child catches on quickly, does not mind losing, and is not intimidated by grown-ups, then go for it.

10. My child has been playing for a few weeks but does not seem to be getting better. How can I help?

Be patient. Chess is a game that takes years to master; a few weeks is barely a blip on the learning curve. There will be many times in a young chess player's development when growth levels off for extended periods, and when a sudden spurt rushes her forward. The key is to make sure your child is constantly stimulated enough by the game to want to study and practice. Improvement will slowly but surely follow.

11. My child is completely hooked and wants to play chess all the time, even during dinner. How can I get him to do other things?

Welcome to the life of a chess parent! A child finding a passion is not a bad thing. It also gives you the leverage to help motivate your child to do other activities. I do not recommend routinely using the threat of taking chess away from your child. Instead, it is much wiser to use the possibility of playing chess as a reward for good behavior.

You should set firm limits on the amount of time your child plays and practices each day. If your child is that interested, however, you should absolutely seek out professional training from a coach. This person will be a close ally in advising your child to fulfill all his other responsibilities. And God bless: You have given your child a gift that will last a lifetime.

12. How soon should my child begin playing in tournaments?

Children can begin playing in tournaments soon after they are comfortable with all the rules. However, the most important factor is a child's personality, as some children handle the stress and challenges of tournaments much better than others. The best guide will be your child's words and attitude. Bring up the topic of tournaments in casual conversation and see how your child responds. Mention, in a hypothetical way, that she might lose all her games and see how she handles that prospect. If she has the right attitude—that it's all about having fun and maybe winning some games—then things should be just fine. You might want to visit a small tournament in your area to familiarize your child with tournament etiquette. Usually, the tournament director will be happy to explain all the basic details you and your child will need to know.

Tournaments can be found online at http://www.uschess.org.

For Educators

1. How do I start a chess club in my school?

The first step is to see if there is an interested faculty member who will oversee the program. Usually there is one teacher in the school who plays chess or thinks a chess club is a good idea. Then, to judge the level of interest that may already exist, create flyers for kids to take home to parents. (An announcement over the PA system as a prelude to this is a good idea.) Create a sign-up sheet and give copies to classroom teachers. This will be your baseline. If the interest is tepid, then start small by having a simple after-school club once a week with your faculty member teaching the kids the basics (see "Recommended Books" for great beginners' books). A more robust response might mean that you need to ask for outside help.

2. Should I get a coach for the students or can I have an interested faculty member teach the group?

This all depends on the skill and motivation of the faculty member. If the person on staff has any chess tournament experience, then without question that is the best solution. However, a trained chess coach can take kids to a level far beyond what an enthusiastic but untrained faculty member can do.

3. Where can I find a good coach?

Unfortunately, once one leaves the highly concentrated urban areas, good coaches are not so easy to find. The simplest thing to do is to contact your local chess club and ask the manager for information on people who coach chess in the area. If this does not produce a satisfactory solution, contact the U.S. Chess Federation at 845-562-8350.

4. How much does a coach cost?

Prices charged by coaches vary widely based on several factors. Grandmasters may charge as little as $50 an hour to as high as $300 an hour in private school settings. Other coaches with high reputations often come with a price tag comparable to grandmaster fees. The normal range for coaches, though, is from $30 to $50 an hour, even in a chess city like New York. In other states, where chess is in less demand and which hold a smaller share of world-class players, the fees tend to be a bit less.

A huge part of the fee charged will also depend on the

type of program being taught. If the school is charging the parents for chess, then the coach will naturally want a big percentage of the gross. If, on the other hand, the program is being completely funded by the school, then the price will tend to be on the lower end.

5. When should my students begin playing in chess tournaments?

The beautiful thing about chess tournaments is that there is something for everybody. Because of the magic of the rating system, kids of every level can be grouped against one another to create fair conditions for all. There are enough beginners' tournaments for new kids to enter.

The real challenge is the emotional readiness of the child. Most very young kids do not like to lose and will pout or even cry at tournaments. The additional stress of playing games that mean more than a regular game at school with friends can sometimes upset the youngest kids. That said, the majority of kids can and do enjoy playing in tournaments, even when the results are not in their favor. The excitement of traveling, the possibility of winning a trophy, and the appeal of making new friends makes the experience one that kids treasure.

B. THE RULES
OF CHESS

Chess is a game for two players, one with the "White" pieces and one with the "Black" pieces. At the beginning of the game, the pieces are set up as pictured below (see later diagrams to identify pieces).

These hints will help you to remember the proper board setup:

1. Opposing Kings and Queens go directly opposite each other.

2. The square on the lower right hand corner is a light one ("light on right").

3. The White Queen goes on a light square, and the Black Queen on a dark square ("Queen on her own color").

♟ THE PIECES AND HOW THEY MOVE

White always moves first, and then the players take turns moving. Only one piece may be moved on each turn (except for castling, a special move that I'll explain later). The Knight is the only piece that can jump over other pieces. All other pieces move along unblocked lines. You may not move a piece to a square already occupied by one of your own pieces. But you can capture an opponent's piece that stands on a square where one of your pieces can move. Simply remove the opponent's piece from the board and put your own piece in its place.

♚ THE KING

The King is the most *important* piece. When he is trapped, his whole army loses. The King can move one square in any direction (an exception is castling, which is explained later). The King may never move into check— that is, onto a square that may be attacked by an opponent's piece.

♛ THE QUEEN

The Queen is the most *powerful* piece. She can move any number of squares in any direction—horizontal, vertical, or diagonal—if her path is not blocked.

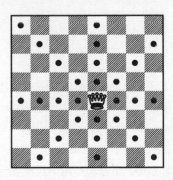

♜ THE ROOK

The Rook is the next most *powerful* piece. The Rook can move any number of squares vertically or horizontally if its path is not blocked.

♝ THE BISHOP

The Bishop can move any number of squares diagonally if its path is not blocked. Note that the Bishop that starts on a light square can only reach other light squares. At the beginning of the game, there is one "light-square" Bishop and one "dark-square" Bishop on each side.

♞ THE KNIGHT

The Knight's move is special. It hops directly from the square it's standing on to its next square. The Knight can jump over other pieces between its old and new squares. Think of the Knight's move as an "L." It moves two squares horizontally or vertically and then it makes a right-angle turn for one more square. The Knight always lands on a square opposite in color from its former square.

♟ THE PAWN

The pawn moves straight ahead (never backward), but it captures diagonally. It normally moves one square at a time, but on its first move it has the option of moving forward one or two squares.

In the diagram, the squares with dots indicate possible destinations for the pawns. The White pawn is on its original square, so it may move ahead either one or two squares. The Black pawn has already moved, so it may move ahead only one square at a time. The squares on which these pawns may capture are indicated by an X.

If a pawn advances all the way to the opposite end of the board, it is immediately "promoted" to another piece, usually a Queen. It may not remain a pawn or become a King. Therefore, it is possible for each player to have more than one Queen or more than two Rooks, Bishops, or Knights on the board at the same time.

Special Moves

♟ CASTLING

Each player may castle only once during a game and only when certain conditions are met. Castling is a special move that lets a player move two pieces at once—the King and one Rook. In castling, the player moves his King two squares to its left or right toward one of his Rooks. On the same turn, the Rook involved is moved to the square beside the King on the opposite side.

Before

After

Before　　　　　　　　*After*

In order to castle, neither the King nor the Rook involved may have moved before. Also, the King may not castle while in check, into check, or past a square that is guarded by an enemy piece ("through check"). Further, there may not be pieces of either color between the King and the Rook involved in castling.

Castling is often a very important move because it allows the King to be placed in a safe location and allows the Rook to become more active.

♟ EN PASSANT

This French phrase is used for a special pawn capture. It means "in passing," and it occurs when one player moves a pawn two squares forward to try to avoid capture by the opponent's pawn. The capture is made exactly as if the player had moved the pawn only one square forward.

In the diagram, one of the Black pawns moves up two squares to the square with the dot. On its turn, the White pawn may capture the Black pawn that just moved by moving to the square marked X. If the player with White does not exercise this option immediately—before playing some other move—the Black pawn is safe from *en passant* capture for the rest of the game. But new opportunities may arise for each pawn in similar circumstances.

♟ ABOUT CHECK AND CHECKMATE

The main goal of chess is to checkmate the opponent's King. The King is not actually captured and removed from the board like the other pieces. But if the King is attacked ("checked") and threatened with capture, it must get out of check immediately. If there is no way to get out of check, the position is a "checkmate," and the side that is checkmated loses.

A King cannot move into check. For example, moving into a direct line with the opponent's Rook if there are no other pieces between the Rook and the King is an illegal move.

If the King is in check, there are three ways of getting out:

1. Capturing the attacking piece.
2. Placing a piece or pawn between the attacker and the King (if the attacker is a Knight, then this is not possible).
3. Moving the King away from the attack. If a checked player can do none of these, he is checkmated and loses the game.

If a player's King is not in check and there is no legal move with any of the pieces, the position is called a stalemate. In this case, the game ends in a draw, or tie.

C. GLOSSARY OF CHESS TERMS

Action chess: A game in which each player has thirty minutes to make all of his or her moves. This form became very popular in the 1990s and is often played at weekend scholastic events.

Adjust: To center a piece on its square. The phrase "I adjust" or *"J'adoube"* must be said before touching any chess piece that one does not intend to move. Otherwise, the player is bound by the touch-move rule to move a piece that has been touched.

Algebraic notation: The most frequently used method for recording chess moves. The files are labeled a to h while the ranks are numbered 1 to 8. Each square is then a meeting point of a letter and number and gets that designation. For example, the square in the lower right-hand corner, from White's point of view, is h1 (letter first, then the number).

Analysis: An extensive examination of the potentially good moves in a given chess position. This process is one of the most important skills for a chess player to master.

Annotation: Written commentary on a past chess game or position, usually done by master players. Annotators will open a window into the nuances behind the moves, and suggest improvements for both sides. Ninety-nine percent of all chess books feature some form of annotation.

Blindfold play: To play without sight of the board. The player calls out his or her moves in one of the popular notations (see **Algebraic notation**), and can only hear the response. The moves are actually played on the board by the opponent or a facilitator. The average person thinks this is a feat almost impossible to do, but some masters have played over forty games at a time blindfolded.

Blitz, also known as **speed chess:** A fast version of chess, played with a clock, where each side typically has five minutes to complete the entire game. If one side's time runs out, the result is a loss except in circumstances where the opponent has nothing left to checkmate with. This form of chess is extremely popular worldwide and is a favorite among the scholastic crowd.

Blunder: An egregious error.

Book moves: Moves that are considered standard in various openings and endgames. Players will often copy book moves without too much thought because the moves have held up in practice. A player who plays an unknown move is said to have "left book."

Brilliancy: A game that involves a series of spectacular moves and ideas.

Bughouse: A variant of chess where two-person teams play against each other on two separate boards. Pieces captured by a player on one board can be used by his or her teammate on the other—another favorite of the scholastic crowd, and this writer, too.

Calculate: To look ahead from a given position in order to figure out the best way to play. Grandmasters can routinely see ten moves into the future of a position, and even more in some situations. Chess-playing computers will calculate millions of positions a minute.

Capture (or take): To eliminate one of your opponent's pieces by moving a piece to the square it was standing on.

Castle: A special move in chess where two pieces—a king and rook—move at the same time. Castling is done by moving the king two spaces to the right or left, and moving the rook from the corner to the square next to it on the other side. Some people mistakenly use the word *castle* to describe the rook.

Center: The four squares that form the geometric center of the chessboard. A wider center includes the sixteen center squares. This area is considered the most critical sector of the board because pieces have maximum mobility here. All chess openings are based on achieving some long-term measure of control over this area.

Check: A move that attacks the king. The side in check must try to get the king out of check. There are three ways to do so: 1. Move to a safe square; 2. Capture the checking piece; 3. Block the line of attack between the king and the checking piece. If none of these options is available, then it's **checkmate.**

Checkmate: A position in which a king is in check and has no way to get out of check. Checkmate comes from the Persian *shah mat,* meaning "The king is dead." It is the word most associated with chess worldwide.

Chess Life: A magazine published by the U.S. Chess Federation.

Clock: A timer with two faces that show the remaining thinking time for both players. After each move, the player presses a button on his or her side of the clock. This stops that time from running and begins the opponent's. If a player's time runs out before making time control—the time limit for that game (see **Time control**)—and this is pointed out by the opposing player, he or she loses the game.

Combination: A series of forcing moves involving a sacrifice. The goal is usually to win material or to checkmate, but some combinations result in a better position.

Correspondence chess: Playing chess by mail, though nowadays, with the advent of the Internet, more players are playing chess online.

Counterplay: A process of going on the offensive when attacked.

Defense: An opening used by Black to counter White's initial moves. The names of defenses, or openings for that matter, can often be confusing. Most players stick to one or two for their entire playing career.

Development: The process of getting pieces and pawns onto more aggressive squares in the opening phase of the game.

Draw: A game that ends without a winner.

Endgame: The last phase of a chess game, marked by a significant reduction of the number of pieces on the board.

En passant: French for "in passing." When a pawn, on its original square, advances two squares, it may be captured by an enemy pawn adjacent to it, as though it had only moved one square. This can only happen on the very next move.

Exchange: A simple trade of forces of equal value. If White were to capture a Black knight, and Black also captured a White knight, both sides would have "exchanged knights."

Expert: A player with a rating of 2000 to 2199, according to the U.S. Chess Federation.

Fianchetto: Italian word meaning to develop a bishop along one of the two longest diagonals on the chessboard.

FIDE: The governing body of world chess. The acronym stands for the Federation Internationale des Eschecs, or International Chess Federation.

FIDE master (FM): An international title bestowed on players by FIDE. It is one level below international master.

File: Any of the vertical rows of squares on a chessboard.

Fish: Slang for a weak player.

Flag: On an analog clock, a small hanging piece that rises as the minute hand approaches the twelve. Even with the rise of digital clocks, players still use the term *the flag fell* when a player runs out of time. Other terms encountered are "You're flag's down" or "You're down."

Fool's mate: The shortest possible chess game, the moves being 1.f3 e5 2. g4 Qh4 mate. White cannot be forced into making these moves so this sort of mate usually only happens as an accident by a very weak player.

Fork: A move where one piece attacks more than one enemy piece and/or pawn.

Gambit: An opening salvo where White offers a pawn or two in order to get an advantage in development or spatial control.

Game score: A record of the moves of a game. This allows players and fans to replay the games from chess players throughout history.

Grandmaster (GM): See **International Grandmaster**.

Hang a piece: To leave a piece where it can be easily captured.

Horse: A mistaken term used by beginners to describe a knight.

Illegal move: A move that is not allowed by the rules of chess. When that happens, the player is obligated to retreat the move and play another. In tournament chess, if the offending move is discovered only after a few moves have been played, a tournament director will try to retrace the moves back to the instant where the mistake took place. (See **Scoresheet**)

International Grandmaster, also known as **grandmaster** or **GM:** The highest title conferred on a player by FIDE.

International Master: A title awarded by FIDE. It is second only to International Grandmaster.

Kingside: The half of the board on which the kings stand in the initial position. From White's vantage point, the thirty-two squares to the right.

Major piece: A queen or rook.

Master, or **National Master:** A player rated between 2200 and 2399 by the U.S. Chess Federation.

Match: A series of games between two players or teams. The phrase *chess match* is often used incorrectly to refer to a single game.

Material: The men on the chessboard at any point in a game, excluding kings. To have a "material advantage" means to have a total of pieces and pawns that is higher than the opponent's. Generally speaking, the side with any material advantage is technically winning, but there are numerous instances to the contrary.

Mating material: Material needed to checkmate a king. This requires at least a queen, rook, or pawn that can "promote." A sole bishop or knight is insufficient to checkmate an opposing king without the opponent's pieces blocking in their own king. In tournaments, if a player's time runs out, his opponent must have mating material in order to claim a win.

Men: Term used to describe both pieces and pawns. An important distinction is that pawns are not pieces.

Middlegame: The phase of the game following the opening. It is an artificial definition used by chess players to denote the stage when the "real" action begins. This is usually after both sides have most of their pieces developed. It ends when most of the pieces are off the board, after which the endgame ensues.

Minor piece: A knight or bishop.

Odds: A method of compensating for different skill levels. Giving material odds means removing one or more pawns or pieces from the board at the start of the game. This practice was popular in the nineteenth century. Nowadays, using a clock to give time odds is more frequent, and usually only in blitz chess.

Opening: The first phase of the game, characterized by the development of the pieces and pawns toward the center of the board. Due to the varied number of ways to begin a chess game, openings have been studied, systematized, and given exotic names. A few of the most popular are the Sicilian Defense, the Ruy Lopez, and the Queen's Gambit.

Over-the-board chess: Chess played face to face. Other ways include correspondence chess and the hugely popular online play.

Patzer: Slang for a weak player.

Perpetual check: A situation in which a player gives an endless series of checks from which the opponent cannot escape. This results in a drawn game.

Piece: All of the chessmen excluding the pawns. In its plural form, it is commonly interchangeable with "chessmen."

Position: The placement of the men on the board at any given point in the game. Good chess players are constantly evaluating the status of their position. The word is often used to refer to either camp—for example, "Black has a good position," or "White's position looks miserable."

Postmortem: A postgame discussion about the important moments from the contest. Players learn a tremendous amount from reviewing the game as mistakes are often found and better moves suggested.

Promotion: What a pawn does on arriving to the last rank. The pawn must be promoted to a piece of choice other than a king. This need not be a piece that has already been captured, which means that there can be as many as nine queens or ten knights on the chessboard at one time. Usually, a player will promote a pawn to a queen as it is the most powerful piece.

Queenside: The half of the board on which the queens stand in the initial position. From White's vantage point, the thirty-two squares to the left.

Rank: Any of the horizontal rows of squares on the chessboard.

Rating: A mathematical measure of chess performance. There are varied rating systems used worldwide, the most respected being the Elo Rating System, named after a math professor who first devised it. A player gains or loses rating points depending on games won or lost. Players gain more points if they defeat higher-rated opposition, but lose more if they lose to weaker opposition. Most scholastic players are in the 800 to 1400 range while most grandmasters will rate from 2500 to 2700. The highest rating ever achieved was by Garry Kasparov at 2851.

Recapture: To capture a piece or pawn that has just captured another.

Resign: To concede defeat in a game before checkmate occurs. A player may lay down the king or say "I resign." This is standard practice in tournaments when a player considers his or her position hopeless. While this is common practice among seasoned tournament players, inexperienced players should never resign as there is always a chance the other player will mess up.

Round robin: An all-play-all tournament. This is common at the higher levels of chess, with an average of ten participants. Most chess tournaments are run on the Swiss System format. Very rare are knockout events, where a losing player gets bumped from the tournament.

Sacrifice: A move in which a player intentionally gives away material (whether for nothing or for a man of lesser value) in order to achieve an important goal. This is considered one of the most skilled, and pleasing, techniques in all of chess.

Scholar's mate: A checkmate that occurs in four moves on f7 or f2 with a queen protected by a bishop. Many beginners fall for it, but experienced players rarely play for quick checkmates.

Scoresheet: A paper on which a record of a game is kept.

Section: A designated group of players within a tournament. Sections may be classified by rating, grade, age, scholastic, etc.

Senior master: The highest national title that can be achieved in the United States. It is conferred on a player who has achieved a rating of 2400 or higher.

Shot: Slang term for a move that stuns the opponent.

Simplification: The process of reducing the material on the board by exchanges. Most often used when a player is ahead in material since it generally makes the game much easier to win.

Simul: Short for "simultaneous exhibition." A special chess event where a strong player takes on many opponents at the same time. The player walks from board to board, moving quickly, while the participants wait for his or her return. Grandmasters can play up to forty opponents very easily, although losses in a couple of games do happen from time to time.

Skittles: Chess for fun. A skittles room is an area where players go to relax between games (although most kids will continue to play even there!).

Space: The total number of squares controlled by the chessmen. The side with more space is often considered to have the advantage.

Stalemate: A position in which a player has no legal move but is not in check. By rule, the game is a draw. The term is often misused to refer to all types of draws.

Strategy: The plan in a given position. Any of various long-term goals that one might seek to achieve in a chess game. **Tactics** are the means by which the objectives are carried out.

Swindle: A clever trap, made by a player with a lost position, that tricks the opponent and changes an almost sure loss to a win or draw.

Swiss System: A type of tournament in which players are paired against each other based on their scores. Unlike a round robin (where all play all, regardless of their scores) or an elimination tournament, players in a Swiss are limited to playing only those players who have the same or close to the same number of points they have. A player who has won three games will be paired, whenever possible, with another player who has won three games. The same applies to players who have lost all their games. One important exception is that players are not allowed to play each other twice.

Tactics: Moves that focus on executing or preventing threats. The study of tactical motifs will repay itself many times over.

TD: Short for tournament director, this is an official trained to run a chess tournament in a manner consistent with the rules and regulations of the national or international federation.

Threat: A move that attempts to gain a significant advantage (such as material, checkmate, or even an important square).

Time control: The time limit in effect for a given game. For example, "40 in 2" means that each side is required to make forty moves in less than two hours. If this is accomplished successfully, then a new time control is put into effect until the game ends. Another popular example is "Game in 30," which means that all the moves must be played in less than thirty minutes per side. "SD/30" stands for Sudden Death in thirty minutes and means the same as "Game in 30."

Time trouble: A situation in which a player has to make a high number of moves in a short period of time to avoid forfeiting the game. Even world-class players have been known to make egregious blunders under these circumstances.

Touch-move rule: The standard practice in chess that states: (1) if you touch a piece, you must move it; (2) once you let go of a piece, you must leave it on that square; and (3) if you touch an opponent's piece, you must capture it. The only exception is if any one of the above acts is illegal by the laws of chess. No serious player plays by any other rules, even in nontournament games. Players are allowed to adjust pieces that have accidentally shifted off the center of squares, but only if preceded by the words *I adjust* or the French equivalent *J'adoube*.

Tournament: A chess event in which participants play more than one opponent. Almost all tournaments are rated and played with a clock.

Trap: A deceptive move meant to ensnare an unsuspecting player.

Unrated: A player who does not have an official rating by the national federation, based on a minimum number of games.

USCF: United States Chess Federation.

Wall chart: Information posted during a tournament showing all the participants, generally ordered by section and rating. Other basic information includes results per round, colors played (Black or White), and opponents.

Zugzwang: German for "compulsion to move"—a position in which a player would be safe if it were the opponent's move, but loses because it's his or her turn to move.

D. RECOMMENDED BOOKS

***Square One* by Bruce Pandolfini**

A great workbook for the under-ten crowd. The book re-inforces the basics with plenty of Q&As, which makes the book a wonderful teaching tool. Pandolfini (played by Ben Kingsley in the chess classic *Searching for Bobby Fischer*) is a well-known chess writer who is famous for reducing complicated material into terms both young and old can understand.

***Bobby Fischer Teaches Chess* by Bobby Fischer**

As simple a book on the basics as there is. For those who may be intimidated at first by complicated-looking chess notation, this book uses arrows to show all the important moves. If someone complains that chess is way too complex, this book will quickly dispel that myth.

***Logical Chess: Move by Move* by Irving Chernev**

One of my all-time favorites. Chernev takes the absolute beginner who knows only the rules and explains fundamental strategy and tactics in a systematic way. After reading this book, most people can begin to call themselves chess players.

The Complete Idiot's Guide to Chess by Patrick Wolff

A lucid and thorough grounding in rules and basic strategy by a grandmaster and former U.S. champion. It's full of information on famous players, the rules of tournament play, chess in cyberspace, and those irritatingly strong chess computers. Also includes a list of some popular chess clubs around the country.

Winning Chess Tactics by Yasser Seirawan and Jeremy Silman

A complete course on tactics by two of the best writers around. The book takes tactics out the realm of the seasoned veteran and explains the subject in simple, clear language. Seirawan is a four-time U.S. champion who is often called upon to provide TV commentary because of his illuminating style. Silman is a well-known author whose more advanced books are a must purchase for any serious chess library.

Winning Chess Strategies by Yasser Seirawan and Jeremy Silman

What they did for tactics, they do for strategy. The topics (and authors) go together like cornflakes and milk.

Comprehensive Chess Course Volume 7: Just the Facts by Lev Alburt and Nikolay Krogius

It's no accident that this book was named 2000–2001 Book of the Year by the Chess Journalists of America. The authors include all the important positions that beginners need to close out a hard-fought game, as well as some interesting practical examples from actual play. This book almost makes other beginning books on the endgame irrelevant.

Classic Books

My System by Aron Nimzovich

I would be remiss not to mention this classic. While it is only to be read after a player has developed a bit of experience with the game, this book has been a hit with generations of readers. It is a bit heavy reading in places, but any effort invested will be well worth it in the end. I must have read this one six or seven times.

How to Reassess Your Chess by Jeremy Silman

An instant classic. Although it was written relatively recently (1993), this book has the feel of one that has been around for decades. Peppered with deep insights on almost every page, the book can make the boast that it can take a devoted reader close to, if not past, the master level. Like a favorite movie, this book should be visited again and again.

Additional Books of Interest

A Parent's Guide to Chess by Dan Heisman; Survival Guide for Chess Parents by Tanya Jones

Written for the parent who wants to dive into the world of tournament chess, both books offer a practical guide of what parents need to know and expect.

Searching for Bobby Fischer by Fred Waitzkin

The book that was made into a movie. A book for a general readership, it describes a father's journey with his enormously talented son through the intense world of competitive chess. While the book is informative and the story engaging, it is Waitzkin's writing that captures the imagination and engages the reader throughout. Even as a chess player, I found it fascinating.

Teaching Life Skills Through Chess: A Guide for Educators and Counselors by Fernando Moreno

Written mainly to help counselors and others interested in child psychology, this book details the various ways in which the author has used chess to help kids handle life's trials.

E. INTERNET RESOURCES

The following are some of the best and most established online portals to the world of chess. Whether you wish to play, purchase instructional books or equipment, or follow the latest news in the world of chess, there is a quality site that brings it to you. These sites,* from what I can tell, are also very respectful to a young audience.

http://www.uschess.org

This site is the home of the U.S. Chess Federation, the official voice of American chess. It has info about tournaments, ratings, scholastic chess, top players, local clubs, latest news, and much more.

http://www.chesscafe.com

This site doubles as the official vendor of books and equipment for the U.S. Chess Federation as well as a sophisticated Internet chess magazine for the serious fan.

*All sites are current as of November 1, 2004.

Other books and equipment may be purchased at:

http://www.wholesalechess.com
http://www.discountchessshop.com
http://www.smartchess.com
http://www.chessusa.com
http://www.allthekingsmenchesssupplies.com/
    online-store/scstore/ index.html

http://www.chessclub.com
One of the most famous sites for players wishing to
play online. While Yahoo and AOL have their own sites,
this one is for the serious enthusiast and one of the few
that top grandmasters the world over frequent on a regular basis. It has a small membership fee that is well worth
the numerous benefits it has to offer.

Other playing servers include:

http://www.playchess.com
http://www.worldchessnetwork.com

http://www.chesscenter.com/twic/twic.html
The original Web site for the latest tournament news.
If a top player is playing anywhere in the world, this site
brings the news on a timely basis.

http://www.thechessdrum.net
The premier Black Web site in the world. If something
of interest is happening anywhere in the African diaspora,
this site is covering it. The site packs scores of player pro-

files along with historical information, beautiful games, interviews, and more.

http://www.chessbase.com

A picturesque site that covers the latest news and human interest stores in the world of chess as well as offering some of the highest quality instructional software on the market. The Chessbase family is most well known for their database of over two million games, their program that allows users to efficiently sift through all the data, their world-class playing engine "Fritz," and their many software tutorials.

For **Maurice Ashley–related** sites, visit:

http://www.mauriceashley.com

http://www.generationchess.com

http://www.chesswise.com

To find out about local chess clubs, visit http://www.uschess.org/clubs

To see a compilation of the studies linking chess and education, visit http://www.psmcd.ca/ftpfolder/BenefitsOfChessinEdScreen2.pdf.

F. THEY ALL PLAY(ED) CHESS

The following list reads like a Who's Who in world history. From Nobel Laureates to musicians, scientists to sports figures, actors to politicians, the game of chess has entertained a broad and prestigious group of fans. The fact that the game is so universally enjoyed by such a diverse body of genius and talent strongly suggests that playing it has some merit. Will your child automatically become one of these greats of history by playing chess? Maybe not, but it can't hurt to give it a shot.

I hope educators will use this list as a way of connecting the skills their students are learning in chess to what they are studying in other areas. One easy way to do this is to assign students a paper based on the question: How did the skills chess teaches help one of the individuals below in their area of expertise? Teachers may also choose from the list themselves based on topics that are currently being taught to the students. As the list shows, it's not just mathematicians and scientists who have benefited from chess over the centuries.

Nobel Laureates

Beckett, Samuel	Literature, 1969
Canetti, Elias	Literature, 1981
Conforth, John	Chemistry, 1975
Debreu, Gerard	Economics, 1983
Einstein, Albert	Physics, 1921
Feynman, Richard	Physics, 1965
Golding, William	Literature, 1983
Harsanyi, John	Economics, 1994
Lewis, Sinclair	Literature, 1930
Kipling, Rudyard	Literature, 1907
Nash, John	Economics, 1994
Pasternak, Boris	Literature, 1958
Robinson, Sir Robert	Chemistry, 1947
Russell, Bertrand	Literature, 1950
Sienkiewicz, Henryk	Literature, 1905
Simon, Herbert	Economics, 1978
Singer, Isaac Bashevis	Literature, 1978
Soddy, Sir Frederick	Chemistry, 1921
Steinbeck, John	Literature, 1962
Yeats, William Butler	Literature, 1923

Sports

Abdul-Jabbar, Kareem	Basketball player
Arrington, LaVar	Football player
Ballesteros, Seve	Masters golf champion
Barnett, Dick	Basketball player

Barrow, Mike	Football player
Becker, Boris	Tennis player
Bouton, Jim	Baseball player
Bruno, Frank	British heavyweight boxer
Bugner, Joe	Heavyweight boxer
Burleigh, Lord	Track star
Cartwright, Bill	Basketball player
Chang, Michael	Tennis player
Elliot, Sean	Basketball player
Gowdy, Curt	Sportscaster
Grace, William	Father of English cricket
Guidry, Ron	Baseball player
Holyfield, Evander	Heavyweight boxer
Johnson, Larry	Basketball player
Jones, Bobby	Golfer
Kastner, Tony	Skier
Knox, Chuck	Football coach
Lendl, Ivan	Tennis player
Lewis, Lennox	Heavyweight boxer
Marshall, Mike	Baseball player
Martin, Curtis	Football player
McEnroe, John	Tennis player
Ovett, Steve	Olympic runner
Powell, Mike	Long-jump world champion
Radjenovic, Boris	Olympic bobsled pilot
Short, Brandon	Football player
Smith, Steve	Basketball player

Tunney, Gene	Heavyweight boxer
Walker, John	Track star
Walsh, Bill	Football coach
Walton, Bill	Basketball player
Winslow, Kellen	Football player
Zatopek, Emil	Olympic runner

Scientists and Mathematicians

De Moivre, Abraham	Mathematician
Erdos, Paul	Mathematician
Euler, Leonhard	Mathematician and physicist
Gauss, Carl Friedrick	Mathematician
Hawking, Stephen	Physicist
Hoyle, Fred	Astronomer
Kapitza, A. P.	Physicist
Lomonosov, Mikhail	Natural scientist
Mendeleyev, Dmitri	Chemist
Moore, Patrick	Astronomer, author
Newton, Isaac	Mathematician
Oppenheimer, Robert	Physicist
Pascal, Blaise	Mathematician
Pauli, Wolfgang	Astronomer
Piccard, August	Physicist, builder of bathyscaphe
Poincaré, Henri	Mathematician
Szilard, Leo	Physicist
Ulam, Stanislaw	Topologist

Film and Television Personalities

Akins, Claude	Actor
Alda, Alan	Actor
Allen, Woody	Director/actor
Barrymore, Lionel	Actor
Baryshnikov, Mikhail	Actor/ballet star
Bergman, Ingmar	Director
Bikel, Theodore	Actor
Bogart, Humphrey	Actor
Boone, Richard	Actor
Booth, Shirley	Actor
Brando, Marlon	Actor
Caesar, Sid	Actor/comedian
Chaplin, Charlie	Actor, silent film star
Coburn, Charles	Actor
Cooke, Alistair	PBS broadcaster
Cosby, Bill	Actor/comedian
Diamond, Dustin	Actor
Dietrich, Marlene	Actor
Downs, Hugh	Actor
Estrada, Erik	Actor
Fairbanks, Douglas	Actor
Falk, Peter	Actor
Farrell, Mike	Actor
Farrow, Mia	Actor
Ferrer, José	Actor, producer, writer
Field, Ted	Producer
Flynn, Errol	Actor
Fonda, Henry	Actor

Forman, Milos	Director
Fox, Michael J.	Actor
Foxx, Jamie	Actor
Gabor, Zsa Zsa	Actor
Hepburn, Katharine	Actor
Hoffman, Kurt	Director
Hope, Bob	Actor/comedian
Huston, John	Director
Jackson, Kate	Actor
Jaffe, Sam	Actor
Johnson, Don	Actor
Jolson, Al	Actor, singer
Jourdan, Louis	Actor
Komack, Jimmy	Producer
Kubrick, Stanley	Director
Leach, Robin	TV talk host
Lee, Belinda	Actor
Letterman, David	TV talk host
Lorre, Peter	Actor
Loy, Myrna	Actor
Martin, Steve	Actor, comedian
Mathers, Jerry	Actor
Matthau, Walter	Actor
McGoohan, Patrick	Actor
Montand, Yves	Actor
Murray, Roseanne	Actor
Newman, Paul	Actor
O'Reilly, Bill	TV host
O'Sullivan, Maureen	Actor
Peppard, George	Actor

Pidgeon, Walter	Actor
Pritkin, Carol	Actor
Quaid, Dennis	Actor
Quinn, Anthony	Actor
Randall, Tony	Actor
Romero, Cesar	Actor
Rossellini, Roberto	Director
St. John, Jill	Actor
Scherer, Gene "Ivan"	Actor
Schwarzenegger, Arnold	Actor
Scott, George C.	Actor
Selleck, Tom	Actor
Sharif, Omar	Actor
Smith, Will	Actor
Stern, Howard	Radio and TV personality
Stewart, Jimmy	Actor
Temple, Shirley	Film child star; U.S. ambassador
Turner, Lana	Actor
Vint, Jesse	Actor
Walston, Ray	Actor
Wayne, John	Actor
Welles, Orson	Actor
Wilder, Billy	Director
Windom, William	Actor

Writers

Amis, Martin	*Money*
Amory, Cleveland	*The Cat Who Came for Christmas*
Asimov, Isaac	Science, science fiction
Balzac, Honoré de	French writer of realist novels
Baum, L. Frank	*The Wizard of Oz*
Bellamy, Guy	*The Secret Lemonade Drinker*
Benedictus, David	*Fourth of June*
Blackmore, R. D.	*Lorna Doone*
Blyton, Enid	Children's books
Borges, Jorge Luis	*The Immortal, The Lie*
Bronowski, Jacob	*The Ascent of Man*
Buchwald, Art	*While Reagan Slept*
Carroll, Lewis	*Alice's Adventures in Wonderland*
Cervantes, Miguel de	*Don Quixote*
Conrad, Joseph	*Lord Jim*
Dickens, Charles	*Oliver Twist*
Dostoevsky, Fyodor	*Crime and Punishment*
Doyle, Arthur Conan	Sherlock Holmes mysteries
Eliot, George	*Middlemarch*
Forster, E. M.	*A Passage to India*
Goethe, Johann Wolfgang von	*Faust*

Goldsmith, Oliver	*The Deserted Village*
Gorky, Maxim	*The Life of Klim Samgin*
Grimm, Jakob	Grimm's fairy tales
Ibsen, Henrik	*A Doll's House*
Jones, James	*From Here to Eternity*
Jonson, Ben	*Every Man in His Humour*
London, Jack	*Call of the Wild*
Mailer, Norman	*The Naked and the Dead*
Melville, Herman	*Moby Dick*
Milne, A. A.	*Winnie-the-Pooh*
Musset, Alfred de	*Lorenzaccio, Poésies Nouvelles*
Nabokov, Vladimir	*Lolita, The Defense*
Orwell, George	*1984, Animal Farm*
Poe, Edgar Allan	"The Tell-Tale Heart"
Porter, William Sydney (O. Henry)	"The Ransom of Red Chief"
Pushkin, Alexander	*The Queen of Spades*
Roget, Peter Mark	Thesaurus
Rushdie, Salman	*Midnight's Children*
Ruskin, John	*The Stones of Venice*
Shakespeare, William	*Hamlet, Macbeth*
Shaw, George Bernard	*Pygmalion*
Stevenson, Robert Louis	*Treasure Island*
Tennyson, Alfred Lord	*The Charge of the Light Brigade*

Tevis, Walter	*Hustler, The Queen's Gambit*
Tolstoy, Leo	*War and Peace*
Vonnegut, Kurt	*Slaughterhouse Five*
Waugh, Evelyn	*Brideshead Revisited*
Wells, H. G.	*The Time Machine*
Zweig, Stefan	*The World of Yesterday*

Musicians

Beecham, Thomas	Conductor
Beethoven, Ludwig van	Composer
Bono	Singer
Borodin, Alexander	Composer and chemist
Bowie, David	Singer
Brodsky, Adolf	Violinist
Brown, Clifford	Trumpeter
Caruso, Enrico	Operatic tenor
Casals, Pablo	Cellist
Charles, Ray	Singer/pianist
Chopin, Frédéric	Composer
Darin, Bobby	Singer
Diamond, Neil	Singer, composer
Dvořák, Antonín	Composer
Elman, Mischa	Violinist
Gillespie, John "Dizzy"	Trumpeter
Goffin, Gerry	Songwriter
Kahn, Leo	Violinist
Lennon, John	Composer, singer

Lill, John	Classical pianist
Madonna	Singer
Marks, Johnny	Composer
Marsalis, Wynton	Composer/trumpeter
Mendelssohn, Felix	Composer
Menuhin, Yehudi	Violinist
Mussorgsky, Modest	Composer
Nash, Graham	Singer, composer
Nelson, Willie	Singer
Oistrakh, David	Violinist
Ono, Yoko	Singer, artist
Persinger, Louis	Violinist
Piatigorsky, Gregor	Cellist
Prokofiev, Sergei	Composer
Reddy, Helen	Singer
Ricci, Ruggiero	Violinist
Rice, Tim	Lyricist
Richter, Sviatoslav	Concert pianist
Rosenthal, Moriz	Concert pianist
Rubinstein, Artur	Concert pianist
Schumann, Robert	Composer
Shostakovich, Dmitri	Composer
Sinatra, Frank	Singer, actor
Starr, Ringo	Drummer
Stern, Isaac	Violinist
Sting	Singer
Strauss, Richard	Composer
Streisand, Barbra	Singer
Ulvaeus, Bjorn	Singer
Verdi, Giuseppe	Composer

Villa-Lobos, Heitor	Composer
Whiteman, Paul	Band leader
Willmers, Rudolph	Concert pianist
Wronski, Tadeusz	Composer and violinist

Politicians and Royals

Abdullah ibn Husain	King of Jordan
Adams, John Quincy	6th U.S. president
Agnew, Spiro T.	39th U.S. vice president
Albert, Prince	Husband of Queen Victoria
Alfonso	King of Spain
Aquino, Cory	Philippine president
Arafat, Yasser	Leader of PLO
Attlee, Clement	British prime minister
Báthory, Stephen	King of Poland
Begin, Menachen	Israeli prime minister
Boleyn, Anne	Mother of Queen Elizabeth I
Bonaparte, Napoleon	Emperor of France
Brandt, Willy	West German chancellor
Brzezinski, Zbigniew	U.S. national security adviser
Canute, King	First king of England
Carter, Amy	Daughter of President Carter

Carter, Jimmy	39th U.S. president
Carter, Rosalynn	Wife of President Carter
Castro, Fidel	Cuban leader
Catherine II	Empress of Russia
Charlemagne	Emperor of Rome
Charles I	King of England
Charles V	French Emperor
Charles VII	King of France
Charles XII	King of Sweden
Churchill, Winston	British prime minister
Conchubhair	King of Ireland
Disraeli, Benjamin	British prime minister
Edward III	King of England
Edward VII	King of United Kingdom
Elizabeth I	Queen of England
Elizabeth II	Queen of England
Farouk, King	King of Egypt
Ferdinand, Archduke	King of Spain
Franco, Francisco	Spanish dictator
Frederick the Great	Prussian monarch
George III	King of England
Gladstone, William	British prime minister
Grouthausen	Minister to Charles XII
Guevara, Che	Revolutionary/guerrilla fighter
Henry VIII	King of England
Ho Chi Minh	President of North Vietnam

Holmes, Oliver Wendell	Supreme Court justice
Isabella	Queen of Spain
Ivan the Terrible	Czar of Russia
Jefferson, Thomas	3rd U.S. president
John I	King of England
Joseph II	Holy Roman Emperor
Kennedy, John F., Jr.	Son of John F. Kennedy
Kissinger, Henry	U.S. secretary of state
La Guardia, Fiorello	Mayor of New York City
Lackland, John	King of England
Landsbergis, Vytautas	Lithuanian president
Lenin, Vladimir	Leader of Bolshevik party
Liebknecht, Karl	German socialist leader
Lincoln, Abraham	16th U.S. president
Louis VI	King of France
Marat, Jean-Paul	French revolutionary
Marcos, Ferdinand	Philippine president
Nasser, Gamal Abdul	Egyptian president
Potemkin	Russian statesman/ prince
Richard I	King of England
Riordan, Richard	Mayor of Los Angeles
Robespierre, Maximilien	French revolutionary
Roosevelt, Teddy	26th U.S. president
Sadat, Anwar	President of Egypt
Salinger, Pierre	JFK's press secretary
Schmidt, Helmut	German chancellor
Sobiesky, Jan	King of Poland

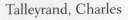

Talleyrand, Charles Maurice de — French diplomat

Tamerlane — Mongol ruler

Tito, Josip — Yugoslav statesman

Trotsky, Leon — Russian revolutionary

William I — King of England

Wilson, Woodrow — 28th U.S. president

Yao Sui — Chinese emperor

Philosophers and Thinkers

Bacon, Sir Francis — Philosopher

Cardano, Girolamo — Philosopher

Diderot, Denis — French encyclopedist

Erasmus, Desiderius — Humanist, theologian

Freud, Sigmund — Psychoanalyst

Jones, Ernest — Psychoanalyst

Keynes, John Maynard — Economist

Leibniz, Gottfried — Philosopher

Lelewel, Joachim — Historian

Machiavelli, Niccolò — Political analyst

Marx, Karl — Political philosopher

Navoi, Alisher — Uzbek poet and sage

Rousseau, Jean-Jacques — Philosopher

Turing, Alan — Computer expert

Voltaire — Philosopher, scientist

Wittgenstein, Ludwig — Philosopher

Artists

Braque, Georges	Painter
Dalí, Salvador	Painter
Doré, Gustave	Book illustrator
Duchamp, Marcel	Painter
Ernst, Max	Painter
Klee, Paul	Painter
Magritte, René	Painter
Matejko, Jan	Painter
Rembrandt	Painter
Repin, Elias	Painter
Villon, Jacques	Painter

Military Leaders

Custer, George	General
Dewey, George	Admiral
Kościuszko, Tadeusz	Commander/strategist
Lafayette, Marquis de	Commander/strategist
Lee, Robert E.	General
McClellan, George	General
Montgomery, Bernard	Viscount
Murat, Joachim	General
Nimitz, Chester	Admiral
Pershing, John	General
Suvorov, Georgii	Commander/strategist
Wróblewski, Walery	General

Religious Leaders

Becket, Thomas	Archbishop of Canterbury
Borromeo, Charles	Bishop of Milan
Graham, Billy	Evangelist
Gregory VI	Pope
Huss, John	Religious reformer
Innocent III	Pope
John Paul	Pope
John Paul II	Pope
Leo X	Pope
Leo XIII	Pope
Luther, Martin	Head of the Protestant Reformation
Richelieu, Armand	Cardinal

Miscellaneous

Anderson, Terry	Captive/hostage
Barnum, P. T.	Circus showman
Casanova, Giovanni	Italian writer, playboy
Culbertson, Ely	Greatest bridge publicist
Davis, Steve	World snooker champion
Dunlap, Erika	Miss America 2004
Franklin, Benjamin	Statesman, inventor
Gates, Bill	Chairman, Microsoft
Hilton, Barron	CEO of Hilton Hotels

Houdini, Harry	Escape artist
Hunter, Charles	World's fastest speaker
Kreskin	Magician
Leary, Timothy	Advocate of the drug LSD
Marceau, Marcel	World's greatest mime
Pulitzer, Joseph	Newspaper publisher
Romack	Magician
Scott, Robert	Explorer
Sevastianov, Vitaly	Soyuz 9 cosmonaut
Strait, Hirum	Magician
Thumb, Tom	Circus performer
Tussaud, Marie	Founder of London wax museum

Infamous

Goebbels, Paul Joseph	Nazi leader
Goetz, Bernard	New York City subway shooter
Hitler, Adolf	Nazi leader
Manson, Charles	Serial killer
Oswald, Lee Harvey	Accused killer of John F. Kennedy

My special thanks to Bill Wall for his comprehensive list at http://www.geocities.com/siliconvalley/lab/7378/famous. htm. I have dramatically changed the list around from alphabetical to thematic to better aid educators. I have also edited out some material I found superfluous.

ABOUT THE AUTHOR

After attaining a number of high-ranking chess titles during the eighties and early nineties, Maurice Ashley was crowned International Grandmaster of chess in 1999, becoming the first (and to this date, only) Black person to capture the game's highest ranking. He has also taught chess online to youth from around the country via America Online, and is the designer of the award-winning CD-ROM chess tutorial *Maurice Ashley Teaches Chess*. He has served as the ESPN commentator on chess matches and has also run the Harlem Chess Center, an after-school haven for young people interested in learning about chess. A sought-after speaker for youth and chess development programs around the country, he has earned numerous citations from various agencies and organizations, including the City Council of New York and the Board of Education of the City of Chicago. He has also appeared in the 2003 PBS and BBC documentary *America Beyond the Color Line*. He lives with his wife and two children in Queens, New York.